GERMAINE

A PORTRAIT OF MADAME DE STAËL

Madame de Staël, by Jean-Baptiste Isabey.

(*Courtesy of the Louvre: photo Giraudon*)

WAYNE ANDREWS

GERMAINE

A PORTRAIT OF

MADAME DE STAËL

LONDON
VICTOR GOLLANCZ LTD
1964

A PORTRAIT OF

MADAME DE STAËL

LONDON

Printed in Great Britain by
Lowe & Brydone (Printers) Ltd., London

FOR LISA

FOR LISA

FOREWORD

WE KNOW, as Lytton Strachey would be the first to observe, too much about Madame de Staël. Too many letters have been published, too many diaries have been exhumed, and too many indispensable monographs have been placed at the disposition of scholars for the story of her life to fall easily into the simple, happy perspective of a work of art.

Nonetheless, I have tried to simplify the life of Madame de Staël. Whenever possible, I have reduced the number of characters on the stage, reasoning that individuals who live on merely in biographical dictionaries deserve to slumber undisturbed. This means that the reader will be disappointed who plans to pass judgment on each and every member of her retinue. Equally disappointed will be the reader who looks forward to a catalog of her lovers.

Something, however, may have been gained by pruning the cast. Madame de Staël may be seen more clearly. Even if she was not one of the great writers of the French language, she was a great personality, and it is her personality that I hope will emerge in this book.

Although immeasurably attractive herself to many men, she won the devotion of the enchanting Juliette Récamier. Too deeply influenced by the rationalistic eighteenth century to be a poet in her own right, she cast a spell on Chateaubriand, one of the supreme masters of poetic prose. Finally, she succeeded in tantalizing the most brilliant mind in Europe, that of Benjamin Constant. Her battle for the possession of Constant unleashed energies even fiercer than those she spent on her duel with Napoleon Bonaparte.

As a novelist, Madame de Staël is no longer read. As a literary critic, she has no more than an historical claim on our attention. It is as an explorer that she will live. *De l'Allemagne*, her report on the Germany of Goethe and Schiller, may be the most challenging invitation ever extended to examine the civilization of another country. She was, of course, no prophet. She could not foresee that Germany would take a turn that would have appalled the poets at the court of Weimar. But her comments on what once was are no less cogent.

She was foolish. She was guilty, on more than one occasion, of favoring men who could not be compared with Chateaubriand or Constant. This is a failing that I hope has not been overemphasized. The biographer who believes he is superior to his subject runs the risk of being no biographer at all, but only a bore.

Her mistakes could be forgiven. She was an adventuress of the type that Guillaume Apollinaire celebrated in *La Jolie Rousse:*

Vous dont la bouche est faite à l'image de celle de Dieu
Bouche qui est l'ordre même
Soyez indulgents quand vous nous comparez
A ceux qui furent la perfection de l'ordre
Nous qui quêtons partout l'aventure

Wayne Andrews

CONTENTS

CONTENTS

GERMAINE

A PORTRAIT OF MADAME DE STAËL

GERMAINE

A PORTRAIT OF MADAME DE STAËL

CHAPTER ONE

THE CHILDHOOD OF
A PERPETUAL CHILD

SHE was a generous woman, daily surprised by the envy of small minds. She swept into drawing rooms the timid had never dared to enter, and there were those who dreaded the gestures that proclaimed her the freest woman in Europe. The envious could not understand that she was not so independent as she seemed. She was endowed, or rather, she was burdened with a mother and a father, and the life she lived was spent in their shadow.

Her mother, so Talleyrand said, had every virtue and only one failing: she was intolerable. This was a notion that would never have occurred to the victim of the epigram. The wife of a banker renowned for his good works, she was the mistress of a universe from which doubt was banished.

The mother of Madame de Staël had not always been so secure. As a young girl, when merely Mademoiselle Suzanne Curchod, the daughter of a pastor in the Canton de Vaud, she had fallen in love with Edward Gibbon. The future historian, then too thin to bear the

3

double chin for which he was ultimately remembered, had been dispatched to Switzerland by his anxious father to cure him of what amounted to a predilection for the Roman Catholic Church. He recovered, so completely that no reader of *The Decline and Fall* needs to be told where his sympathies lay.

In Switzerland Gibbon expressed something approaching an interest in Suzanne. "To tell you," he wrote her in the fall of 1757—she was then eighteen and he twenty—"that the week I spent without you seemed a century would be true—but that would be using a threadbare phrase."

Gibbon's concern for Suzanne did not survive his return to England. "I hesitate, from the apprehension of ridicule, when I approach the delicate subject of my early love," he wrote in his autobiography. "The personal attractions of Mademoiselle Suzanne Curchod were embellished by the virtues and talents of the mind. Her fortune was humble, but her family was respectable: her mother, a native of France, had preferred her religion to her country; the profession of her father did not extinguish the moderation and philosophy of his temper, and he lived content with a small salary and laborious duty in the obscure lot of Minister of Crassy, in the mountains that separate the Pays de Vaud from the County of Burgundy.

"In the solitude of a sequestered village," Gibbon went on, "he bestowed a liberal, even learned education on his only daughter; she surpassed his hopes by her proficiency in the sciences and languages; and in her short visits to some relations at Lausanne, the wit and beauty and erudition of Mademoiselle Curchod were the theme of universal applause.

"The report of such a prodigy awakened my curiosity; I saw and loved. I found her learned without pedantry, lively in conversation, pure in sentiment and ele-

4

gant in manners; and the first emotion was fortified by the habits and knowledge of a more familiar acquaintance. She permitted me to make her two or three visits at her father's house: I passed some happy days in the mountains of Burgundy; and her parents honorably encouraged a connection which might raise their daughter above want and dependence. In a calm retirement the gay vanity of youth no longer fluttered in her bosom: she listened to the voice of truth and passion, and I might presume that I had made some impression on a virtuous heart. At Crassy and Lausanne I indulged my dream of felicity; but, on my return to England, I soon discovered that my father would not hear of this strange alliance, and that, without his consent, I was myself destitute and helpless."

Gibbon was the comfortable son of a demanding man: he behaved accordingly. "After a painful struggle I yielded to my fate; the remedies of absence and time were at length effectual, and my love subsided in friendship and esteem."

The historian could ward off the approach of passion, but he was always tempted by prose. "I sighed as a lover, I obeyed as a son," he recalled. "My wound was insensibly healed by time, absence, and the habits of a new life; and my cure was accelerated by a faithful report of the tranquility and cheerfulness of the lady herself."

Here Gibbon was not telling quite the truth. "I have had greater griefs, but none that I felt more keenly," Suzanne could not restrain herself from writing him. "Please tell me that you are not totally indifferent." That he was indifferent was made plain by his silence; the only sign of life he showed in four years was the sending of a copy of his first book, an essay on the study of literature, which he happened to have written in French.

5

In her anxiety the by now fatherless girl appealed to a pastor who in turn appealed to Jean-Jacques Rousseau. "The coldness of Mr. Gibbon gives me a bad idea of his character," wrote Rousseau after examining his French. "I have read his book again. He wants to be clever; it is a mistake. Gibbon is not my sort of man. I can't believe that he's the sort who would suit Mademoiselle Curchod."

Suzanne, who finally reached this very conclusion, made the best of her situation by becoming a governess. By 1764 she was following her profession in Paris. Her employer, she discovered, was engaged to a young but intelligent banker by the name of Jacques Necker.* This was a fact that did not discourage the former fiancée of Gibbon. She admired Necker and she married him. The banker's original choice was notified by letter —after the event.

The son of a Prussian who settled in Geneva, teaching public and private Germanic law, eventually becoming an elder of the city, Necker commanded at an early age the respect of the masters of the money market. At sixteen he went to work for the banker Isaac Vernet. At eighteen he was transferred to the Paris branch of the house, and proved so competent that when Vernet retired in 1762, he was made, at thirty, a partner in the new firm headed by Vernet's nephew Thélusson. The negotiations that led to the end of the Seven Years' War in 1763 offered opportunities that Necker did not neglect. Those in the know heard that he bought up Canadian contracts at 30 per cent and sold out at par. Rumor had it he made no less than 1,800,000 pounds out of the signing of the Peace of Paris.

Suzanne worshipped her husband, but not merely

* The second E in Necker is silent. So his descendants pronounce the name.

6

for his skill as a financier. "From the date of his birth Monsieur Necker was unique in every respect," she declared. "In appearance he resembles no one. The shape of his face is extraordinary. His genius and his amiability are so telling that no one can give him a good look without sensing both these traits. Indeed a glance is sufficient for any sensitive person to melt with admiration. There is something so delicate and so ethereal about his eyes that one is instantly reminded of a painting of an angel."

Not everyone, of course, could appreciate his true worth. "I have often noticed," she added, "when I came to meditate on the generosity and the public spirit of Monsieur Necker that his moral standards were too high to be of interest to other men." Nor should anyone be surprised to hear that exaggeration was a vice he could not condone. "He had only to examine his own heart and mind to know the meaning of grandeur."

This was not all. *"Monsieur Necker peut dire,"* she claimed, *"mon talent à moi, c'est le génie."*

Since the banker was guilty of permitting the publication of these tributes from his wife, the point must be made that he was respected outside of his home. In 1768 he was made Minister of Geneva in Paris, and the firm he directed was so flourishing that in 1772 he resigned, free for the rest of his life from financial burdens. As Suzanne put it, he "quit the business at a time when he could have made ten times more money, simply because he was bored by a kind of work that was neither novel nor attractive."

A eulogy of Colbert that he composed the year after he retired won him a prize from the French Academy. This was recognition, even if Voltaire was unimpressed. "Do you really want me to tell you, Madame," he wrote his good friend Madame du Deffand, "whether I am pleased by a work in which there is as much bad as

7

good, as many obscurities as there are clarities, as many inept phrases as there are correct expressions, and as much exaggeration as there is truth?"

Voltaire could criticize his prose, but few could argue with the banker over public finance. When Turgot, who had fought for drastic and unpopular reforms, was dismissed as Comptroller-General in the spring of 1776, Necker was a candidate for the position. He was not made Director-General until the summer of 1777, perhaps because it was feared he would propose measures equally stern. This is hardly the place for a critical analysis of Necker's financial policies on the eve of the French Revolution, but it may be said that he introduced certain indispensable economies, set up a fund of half a million pounds to begin the liquidation of the arrears of the government, and launched a lottery to bring in other funds. All this he accomplished while promising to provide for all of the pensions. In 1781, after publishing his famous *Compte-rendu* of the state of France's finances, and indicating his lack of sympathy with the nation's involvement in the American Revolution, he was sent away. "I accept your resignation," wrote Louis XVI. "I have had a certain respect for your ability, but your mischievous mind could not please me."

Even when out of favor, the banker had his consolations. In his third year out of office he purchased the estate of Coppet near Geneva. A comfortable home rather than a true château, Coppet was pleasantly situated on the shores of the lake, even if no advantage whatever was taken of the view.

In the meantime his wife had opened a salon in Paris. Necker, she made plain, "likes dull people because of the contrast with his own brilliance." This may be one reason why many of Madame Necker's guests have sunk into the obscurity of the biographical dictionaries. However, d'Alembert was one of the philosophers who came to call. Another was Diderot, whose son-in-law happened to be unemployed at the time. Diderot's presence alarmed the pastor who watched over Suzanne's spiritual life, but she was ready with an answer. "I live, it is true," she wrote him, "amid a great number of atheists. But their arguments have never touched my mind." Furthermore, she could point to the valuable reforms she had introduced in the management of hospitals.

She seldom referred to her greatest accomplishment, the birth on April 22, 1766, of her only child, Anne-Louise-Germaine.

"She is nothing, absolutely nothing compared to what I wanted to make of her," Suzanne once complained. This was true. As impetuous as her mother was calculating, Germaine was a constant threat to the scenery her mother had raised with infinite pains.

She was not a beautiful child, nor was she a beautiful woman. The most devoted of her lovers admitted that her complexion was poor and that she was substantial rather than graceful. But her bosom, he reported, was superb, and her blue eyes—they later darkened—were the most beautiful in the world. And even though her hands were too long, her arms were handsome. Her voice was sweet; when it broke, it was enchanting. Once she was animated, and she often was, she was irresistible.

Her mother, who was understandably anxious to improve her, saw to it that her education was distinguished. She was taught to dance, but was not allowed to romp. She could recite Thomson's *Seasons* before she could tell one flower from another. She had to hide away to play at kings and queens with her paper dolls. In her excitement at that innocent but forbidden game the dark-haired girl would twirl in her fingers a scrap of paper, a mannerism that she never outgrew.

She made an honest effort to be a dutiful child. At ten, aware of her parents' pleasure in the occasional visits from Edward Gibbon, she offered to marry him so that her mother and father might continue to enjoy his conversation. But at thirteen she suffered what appeared to be a nervous breakdown, and on the advice of a famous doctor was sent to the countryside at Saint-Ouen to recover from her mother's ambition.

"My father thinks more of my happiness on earth," she said later, "my mother of my happiness in the world to come." This was made evident one evening when Madame Necker strode into the dining room to find her husband and daughter dancing around the table. Madame Necker uttered not a word, but her husband and her daughter immediately sat down to dinner, ashamed.

Very likely Germaine was recalling this incident when she wrote, long afterward, that Madame Necker was "a woman of the highest moral standards." Terrified as a child of her mother, she found her salvation in adoring her father. His mind was absolutely pure, but he could be absolutely forgiving. In a eulogy printed at his death she went on to say that he loved glory alone. "There is something celestial about glory," she insisted. "Glory is the dividing line between our hopes of heaven and our life on earth." Her admiration was sincere for the sermons he published under the title of *Cours de morale religieuse*. There were those, she admitted, who wondered at a banker's straying so far from profit and loss, but she knew that as a stylist he could be compared to Bossuet. Only once did she indicate that she could look on her father as a mortal. "We all yawn in church," she confessed after revealing that her love for him was a form of religious worship.

These were the opinions of a perpetual child, whose

parents were so important that the laws of perspective were forever suspended. From no matter what angle Germaine was observed, and in no matter what year, her mother and father loomed larger than life, two relentless statues.

At fifteen Germaine was so precocious that she wrote a dissertation on Montesquieu's *Esprit des lois*, not to mention an anonymous letter to her father rendering her opinion of the *Compte-rendu*. At eighteen she was so celebrated that the fastidious English millionaire William Beckford could not resist sending her a copy of his first travel book, *Dreams, Waking Thoughts, and Incidents.*

This was in 1784, and Beckford had not yet erected his incredible Gothic castle at Fonthill. Nor had he begun the composition of *Vathek*, a Gothic tale written in a French so pure that even Mallarmé would be charmed. But he was already a person of taste: Mozart had been hired to teach him to play the piano.

Germaine met the challenge. She was positive, she wrote him, that he was a native of no less a volcano than Mount Aetna, and she invited him to dinner at her parents' house in Paris. Gardel was to dance that day; Piccini would lead the music; Marmontel and the Abbé Raynal would represent the world of letters.

Beckford accepted the invitation, to find that his admirer was a prisoner.

"Lady Clermont often said to me—Keep aloof from Madame Necker's parties if you possibly can—They won't suit you," he wrote his cousin Louisa. "O that I had followed this excellent advice—but there is no resisting fate. . . . I went early, according to summons, and found Gardel and two of his vice-gerents, the slimmest of the slim, each armed with his slender kit, Piccini at the harpsichord and Marmontel and the Abbé Raynal acting the part of the audience. Mademoiselle

11

pounced down upon me the moment I entered and we
began dancing menuets, then followed a gavotte, which
though I performed, as I flattered myself, in my best
style,—did not exactly delight Gardel, who took the
liberty of observing that I rose much higher into the
air than was at all necessary. This exhibition ended, another pounce from Mademoiselle brought me to the
harpsichord, where sat Piccini like a king on his
throne. He accompanied me admirably—much less, I
believe, to his satisfaction than mine, for all he said
was—'I perceive you have heard Pachierotti.' It was
next Mademoiselle's turn to display her musical abilities,
which she did with a vengeance, for she sang incompar-
ably out of tune from the first note to the last of the
grand aria in Piccini's *Didon*. He said nothing, but
looked daggers—his most animated pupil had scarcely
quavered to the last roulade, when the great doors of
the grand saloon flying open discovered a synod of
sallow literati in full court dress, and a row of long-
waisted pink and yellow dowagers, all seated on fau-
teuils composed of the stiffest tapestry, all taking de-
liberate pinches of snuff at frequent intervals, and all
determined to cross examine poor unfortunate me. . . .
In this exemplary task they were aided and abetted by
Buffon, de Lalande, and a host of savants their literary
confessors. . . .

"The dinner," Beckford complained, "was more unc-
tuous than the discourse. . . . Of the whole formid-
able party assembled at table, the master of the house
himself was the least husky and wearisome. . . . I
never beheld any mortal being more complacently self-
satisfied. It does one good to witness the serene and
happy attention with which he listens to all the fine
things his flatterers and satellites (still a numerous
band) are perpetually declaiming to his glory and
praise. . . . When he has just received a well-turned

compliment his mouth becomes as round as the letter O and he appears as if on the point of whistling a bulfinchish reply. His pedantic, domineering consort is a very different sort of personage—just such a one as Molière would have gloried in—half Précieuse-Ridicule and half Comtesse d'Escarbagnas."

The scene was now approaching its inevitable end.

"Being . . . as thirsty as the deserts of Arabia," the English millionaire continued, "I begged earnestly for a very large goblet of water. I happened to be seated by Madame in the very center of her magnificent saloon. The goblet was brought me. I had scarcely begun quaffing it when she screamed out—'Monsieur, in these cases it is the etiquette to rise from your seat, and take your glass of water at the distance of at least two or three paces.' 'Is it so indeed, Madam,' answered I, 'I beg ten thousand pardons—I will immediately retire'—and so I did, but my foot slipping *accidentally* (or the reverse, whichever you like best to conjecture) the whole remaining contents of the capricious goblet fell into Madame's richly brocaded lap. I leave you to figure to yourself her angry gestures, the general surprise, the general consternation, and the lightning-like swiftness with which I darted to the door of the apartment.

"It had hardly closed upon me, when it was reopened by Mademoiselle . . . assisted by Marmontel—and followed by her father lamenting the catastrophe which had just taken place and beseeching me to return and hear explanations. None would I hear—none would I accept. I ran down the stairs without looking behind me, and never intend to run up them again. So help me providence!"

And so Beckford made good his escape from the Neckers. For Germaine flight was impossible.

CHAPTER TWO

WITH A PASSION APPROACHING MY OWN

"I HAVE never been loved," Germaine once observed, "with a passion approaching my own." This was probably true. She was not easily pleased, and she may have frightened more suitors than she attracted when her parents began planning for her marriage. The task of the Neckers was difficult: even if she had not been so demanding, the proper husband in Catholic France for a Calvinist was hard to discover.

For a time the Neckers believed that William Pitt might be suitable for their daughter. Then they realized that she could not live in England; she made that plain. "Why did this wretched England have to turn my own mother against me?" she asked in her diary. "I am sorry I haven't linked my fate with a great man. That is the only glory on earth for a woman—it lifts a woman to the heights. . . . But could I consent to live in England? No. Such is not my destiny. I am the daughter of Necker, I am bound to him, Necker is my name, and I intend to bear the name of Necker even after I've left my father's house. I shall be worthy of the honor."

The Swede who became her husband was the last person to comprehend her particular ambition, but he was available, so available that he waited nearly seven years for the privilege. As early as 1779, when he set out from Paris for Stockholm bearing the drawings of the Petit Trianon—a present from Marie-Antoinette to Gustavus III—this prudent adventurer set his hopes on Germaine. To his dismay the Neckers were more than prudent. If he intended to marry their daughter, he must first be appointed the Swedish ambassador to France.

This was a suggestion that Marie-Antoinette approved of. "Monsieur le Baron de Staël, whom I've already mentioned, is very well liked and highly regarded in this country," she advised Gustavus III in the spring of 1781. "I do not doubt that we should be happy to see him established here in Your Majesty's service."

But the king of Sweden was slow to make up his mind, and in the spring of the following year the Swedish ambassador at the moment, the Comte de Creutz, did his best to further Staël's chances. "If Your Majesty," wrote Creutz, "designed to let Monsieur de Staël assume my position, we could arrange for him to come into one of the greatest fortunes in Europe. One of the motives that might determine Your Majesty to grant him this favor would be the advantage of having among the Swedish nobility a family sufficiently powerful to make a certain impression at court and in the capital as well, for Mademoiselle Necker's income, 500,000 pounds no less, would be the equivalent in Sweden of that of Monsieur de Soubise, the greatest and richest lord of the court of France. Our nobility," Creutz pleaded, "is really too poor. . . . But Your Majesty must come to a decision, for Mademoiselle Necker is sixteen and a half, and her parents won't delay in disposing of her."

Still the king hesitated. In 1783, when Creutz was recalled, Staël was humiliated to learn that he was not appointed in his place. "All the hopes that I have entertained for my marriage are fading," he wrote Gustavus, "for Monsieur Necker most certainly won't bestow his daughter on a man who seems to have lost both the good will and the confidence of his master."

"What I want is Tobago," the king informed Staël, referring to an island in the West Indies for which he had developed an appetite. "If you succeed in this, using your prestige, your tact, and the desire you may be able to arouse in the queen of France to justify her recommendation by the success of such an important negotiation, you may become my ambassador. But if you don't get Tobago (for Tobago is what I am after) I must tell you in all frankness that you will have to get along with the title of minister plenipotentiary and give up all hope of the embassy. Now it is up to you to work out your own salvation."

To add to Staël's difficulties, Necker laid down certain conditions of his own. In addition to being appointed ambassador for life, Staël would have to draw a pension of 25,000 francs in the event he lost the position. Furthermore, he would have to win the Order of the Polar Star and receive the title of count, so that Germaine could not be confused with a certain Baronne de Staël who did not enjoy a good reputation. Nor was this all. He was never to have the right to take his wife to Sweden without her consent. Finally, Marie-Antoinette would have to give her formal approval to the match.

There was a threat of a deadlock in the discussions as late as the summer of 1785, when Madame de Boufflers, who had cultivated both Rousseau and the king of Sweden, wrote Gustavus that "if Your Majesty does not confer the ambassadorship for life, there will be no wedding for the Baron de Staël, and his only conso-

16

lation will be that he caused a fleeting sensation, with the drawback that he ran up 20,000 francs in debts for his establishment in Paris, and for Your Majesty's visit to the city."

In the end a compromise was reached. The Order of the Polar Star was denied the bridegroom and so was the title of count. Tobago was withheld, but the king declared himself satisfied with the adjacent island of Saint-Barthélemy.

On the 14th of January, 1786, Germaine, who was not yet twenty, was married in the chapel of the Swedish embassy to the Baron, who was seventeen years her senior. He was handsome, and she knew it; she also knew that he had the handsomeness of a man who would never acquire a personality. Her husband did not even know how to dance, she recorded in her diary shortly before the wedding day. "He is a perfectly nice man," she wrote, "who won't say anything silly, or do anything wild, but . . . My father all of a sudden said to him, 'Come now, I'll show you how to dance with a girl you're in love with.' In spite of his waistline, in spite of his age, his eyes, those charming eyes of his, and his nimble feet made me feel how much he loved me, how graceful he was, and how much alive. Great Gods! If I could only describe the shrinking of my heart at that moment. I couldn't keep it up. I fled to a corner of the room and I burst into tears."

"My dear Mama," Germaine had announced on the morning of the wedding, "I won't be coming home to you tonight." Madame de Boufflers was not a witness to this scene, but she suspected the worst when she wrote Gustavus. "I would like Staël to be happy, but I have no such hope. His wife has been educated according to the highest principles, it is true, but she has no knowledge of the world, and she has been so spoiled that it would be quite a feat to make her realize what

17

she's missing. . . . She's more sure of herself than
anyone I've seen of her age and in her position. If she
were a little less spoiled by all the incense they've
burned for her, I'd have tried to give her some advice."
Madame de Boufflers might well have hesitated before attempting to improve Germaine's mind. Germaine's father was at last enjoying the prestige which
he had long felt was due him. In the spring of 1787
he was exiled twenty leagues from Paris for presuming
to criticize the policies of Calonne as finance minister,
but by the fall of 1788 he was back in power in Calonne's place. The French Revolution was about to
begin, and Necker was playing an honorable if somewhat exciting role in precipitating events that astonished the world of Madame de Boufflers. He encouraged
the summoning of the States General; he was not averse
to the double representation of the Third Estate; he
even permitted the orders to vote in common. He was
dismissed for his independence of thought on July 11,
1789, but the storming of the Bastille three days later
brought him back to the finance ministry on the 16th.
"All France took his dismissal to be a public calamity,"
Germaine recorded. He was to resign his post in the
fall of 1790 after expressing his distrust of the assig-
nats or revolutionary paper money, but he had his claim
on the admiration of the people. In the winter of 1789,
when the nation was faced with a wheat famine, he lent
half his personal fortune to the royal treasury; what
other financier could have performed in this style?
This was electric news to Germaine, who felt free
to play on a stage outside her home. She had made a
certain impression on Jacques-Antoine-Hippolyte Guibert, a middle-aged count who at one time succeeded in
introducing certain reforms in the French Army. Guibert was an ingratiating man: he succeeded, all too
well, in pleasing Julie de Lespinasse, the confidante

of Voltaire's correspondent, Madame du Deffand. For years Julie pursued him with passionate love letters. These have been admired by those who treasure the evidence of unrequited affection; to Guibert they were a nuisance. In an effort to drive Julie out of his mind, he once composed a polite paragraph in praise of "Zulmé," who was none other than Germaine. "Her features were emphatic rather than delicate," he admitted. "But here was a woman who could rise above the fate of her sex."

There is not the stuff of passion in these remarks, and it is just possible that Guibert was surfeited by his brush with Julie de Lespinasse. But Germaine, searching for the response to her lyric gifts, could not deny herself the satisfaction of a flirtation. After Guibert's death she celebrated his virtues in a eulogy whose sobriety may indicate that she asked for more than he cared to give. "The profound admiration of M. de Guibert for my father, his veneration of my mother, all this interested me," she recorded. He worshipped at the same altar that she did; that, and his advancing years, made their friendship natural and inevitable.

But if Guibert was not a man to take flame, he was a convenient guest, and the thought that she was entertaining him was enough to drive Staël to distraction. "You must forgive me for enjoying the pleasure of this world," Germaine pleaded with her husband. "I don't overdo it, and if you loved me less, you might be more inclined to do me justice, for I am the most reasonable person in the world." She was disappointed when the Baron opened one of her letters to the Count. "Do you intend," she asked, "to poison the happiness which we should be enjoying by indulging in inexcusable jealousy?"

She was willing to confess that she was fond of Guibert's company. "I am a loving nature, and extremely sensitive; sometimes, when I am alone, the emptiness of my heart fills my eyes with tears. I am younger than you; at my age, one feels the need to be loved, and when one's soul is pure, one cannot be guilty of a desire that a virtuous woman would condemn."

The birth of her first child, Edwige-Gustavine, on the 29th of July, 1787, drew Germaine and her husband no closer. The little girl died at eight months, and her mother went on to complete an essay on Rousseau. She also went on to find friends who were far more congenial than Guibert. She later wrote that the three men of whom she was most fond when nineteen or twenty were Mathieu de Montmorency, Charles-Maurice de Talleyrand-Périgord, and Louis de Narbonne-Lara

Mathieu de Montmorency, who died on Good Friday, 1826, while at prayer before the cross, was a man whose passion was soon spent. Although he consented in his old age to become Foreign Minister of France, the Catholic religion was a more endearing subject than the machinations of statesmen or the demands of women. This had not always been so. His piety dated from the hour his brother was guillotined in the Revolution. And his devotion to the Church did not approach that of a fanatic. He watched benignly over Germaine; he could forgive her errors, if not those of her admirers.

Charles-Maurice de Talleyrand-Périgord, consecrated bishop of Autun in the year the Revolution was launched, was not a religious man. His own mother, thinking of his love affairs, was puzzled by the notion of a miter on his brow. Louis XVI reassured her. "It will improve him," he announced. Possibly it did, but he broke the bank not once but twice at a gambling house immediately after celebrating Mass, and early in 1791 resigned from the Church. His interests lay elsewhere. "You know," he was fond of saying, "one simply has to be rich." He always was; his club foot was no hindrance when it came to contemplating investments. "I have found out," Talleyrand observed, "that certain people think there is something wrong about accepting positions in times of crises and revolutions, when the absolute good is impossible of achievement. It has always seemed to me that there was something superficial in that way of looking at things. In the affairs of this world, the present moment is not the only one to be considered. *What is* really doesn't amount to much, if one doesn't stop to think that *what is* produces *what will be*, and to tell the truth, if you want to get anywhere, you have to keep moving."

Keep moving he did, and Germaine was impressed by his progress. She could enjoy his wit; for a long time she was entertained by his want of principle. She had, after all, been dreadfully familiar with principles in her father's house.

Although Louis de Narbonne-Lara could not pretend to be as amusing as Talleyrand, he was charming, and, what was almost as significant, was the victim of the gossipmongers. To Germaine this was an additional claim on her affections. To Gouverneur Morris, who had been in Paris bidding for tobacco contracts long before he was appointed Minister to France, this gossip was gospel. Nursing the scandal as carefully as if it had been a draft on the best Dutch bankers, he wrote George Washington that "Monsieur de Narbonne is said to be the son of Louis XV by Madame Adélaïde his own daughter, and one of the present king's aunts. Certain it is that the old lady, now at Rome, has always protected and befriended him in the warmest manner. In the beginning of the Revolution he, a great anti-Neckerist though the lover *en titre* of Madame de Staël . . . was not a little opposed to the Revolution, and there was afterward some coldness between him and the Bishop, partly on political grounds, and partly because he (in common with the rest of the world) believed the bishop to be well with his mistress. By the by, she tells me that this is not true and of course I who am a charitable man believe her."

The Comte de Narbonne had been careless, even before his ancestry became a tidbit for Gouverneur Morris's correspondence. After making a sagacious marriage with the daughter of the president of the parliament of Rouen, he had fallen violently in love with an actress of the Comédie Française and was the father of her child, born after a brief holiday in England. All of this Germaine was willing to forgive.

Monsieur de Staël, who was on the eve of falling in love with an actress all his own, twenty-six years his senior, chose this moment to play once again the role of the injured husband. Narbonne, he insisted, should be forbidden his house. With this Germaine could not agree. "As to the dozen—or half-dozen hours that I have spent with him," she wrote the Baron, "it would be better for you to learn the facts than to insult me. You go on to say that you haven't run me out of the house; it seems to me that you told me that you didn't care to see Monsieur de N. any longer, and I believe that you understand that I, knowing that my heart is pure, have the courage to stand by my decision in the face of injustice. . . . I am quite fond of Monsieur de N., but not a word of what you say about him is true."

Toward the end of November, 1790, she was again proving her innocence to her husband. "You tell me," she wrote, "that Monsieur de Narbonne has spent five days at Coppet. That's one of the thousand and one lies you've been swallowing. He couldn't possibly have come, and there is no danger of his coming; he neglects me dreadfully."

She was once more a mother when she drafted that

letter; on August 31 Auguste de Staël had come into the world. Seventeen years later the Maréchal de Castellane, who was a reasonably well-informed man, noted in his diary that Auguste was clever and rather handsome. "He looks like Comte Louis de Narbonne. But there is no point in questioning the virtue of Madame de Staël."

Her husband, who was uneasy on this very point, was having his own troubles by the fall of 1791. "My wife," he informed a friend, "is causing me no end of worry, and neither my father- nor my mother-in-law is of any help to me. . . . The state of my finances is desperate. I owe about 60,000 pounds; neither my wife nor her parents know anything about this debt, and the secret must be kept at any cost."

Germaine might have ferreted out the true state of his finances if she had not been following with unconcealed eagerness the progress of the Revolution. The extent of the incompetence of Louis XVI had been revealed that summer, when he was captured at Varennes in the act of fleeing the country. Before the summer was over, the emperor in Austria and the king of Prussia met at Pilnitz to agree on immediate action in the event of an attack by France. On September 14, Louis XVI swore an oath to the new French constitution, under which the clergy were to be treated as civil servants and suffrage was granted—to those who met the requisite property qualifications. But did the allegiance of a weak king to an untried government mean an end to the strivings of the French people? Germaine could not be sure.

Of one thing, however, she was certain. "No revolution in a great country," she believed, "can possibly succeed unless it be launched by the aristocracy. The common people play a part later on, but they can't deal the first cards."

In the very beginning Narbonne played no part at all; he was not even a member of the Constituent Assembly that had laid the foundation for the new constitution. But he had been a commander of the national guard in Franche-Comté, and that summer he headed the guards who quelled a republican riot. Germaine began to be hopeful.

By November Marie-Antoinette recognized that the wife of the Swedish ambassador was a determined woman. "Madame de Staël is doing all she can for Monsieur de Narbonne," she wrote her good friend Fersen. "I've never seen a plot thickening like this before, nor a more complicated one."

On December 7, 1791, Marie-Antoinette understood that the game was up. "The Comte Louis de Narbonne is finally Minister of War," she wrote again to Fersen. "How glorious this must be for Madame de Staël, and what a pleasure it must be for her to have the Army in her hands. . . . If only some day I can prove to all these scoundrels that I was not their dupe."

Germaine may not have had Marie-Antoinette on her mind. She had found an interesting lover, and she had led him to do interesting things. Nine days after Narbonne's appointment, Gustavus III recalled her husband to Stockholm. For once she was enjoying something like freedom.

CHAPTER THREE

NOTHING HUMAN IS ALLOWED TO BE PERFECT

———————◆———————

"*C'est la liberté qui est ancienne, et le despotisme qui est moderne,*" Germaine sincerely believed, and the epigram could explain her concern for the French Revolution. Whether Narbonne shared her ideals is open to question. He was too charming to be important; he could not even impress Louis XVI. He lectured the king on the folly of encouraging the émigrés who were gathering in Germany, and was dismissed for his trouble on the 9th of March, twenty-four hours after Lafayette and Rochambeau had intervened on his behalf.

Germaine never left off hoping that the Revolution could be led by reasonable men, even though cool and calculating politicians were waiting for their cues. One of these men was Robespierre. When war was declared on Austria on April 20, he argued that this was a false move, a symptom of a state of mind more serious than mere impatience. But the war was welcomed on both the left and the right, by those whose only aim was to destroy the monarchy and by those who lived for the day the Revolution would be strangled. Confusion was inevitable; so were the initial defeats of the French armies.

Maddened by the disgraces in the field, the men and women of the Faubourg Saint-Jacques and the Faubourg Saint-Antoine refused to be reasonable; they invaded the Tuileries on the 20th of June, and the humiliated king donned a revolutionary cockade. A month later came the solemn declaration of danger to the nation, and the power of the Commune, or revolutionary government of Paris, threatened that of the Assembly. On the 10th of August the Tuileries was overrun by the mob, the king was "suspended" until the convocation of a national assembly in September, and the Commune of Paris became the master of France.

Germaine could not consent to be merely a spectator of these scenes. As early as July she had written an anxious letter to a friend of the royal family. "Here is my plan," she announced, "which can be carried out in three weeks, if the first steps are taken in the next two days. There is a piece of land for sale near Dieppe. I'll buy it. I'll bring along on each trip to my property a man I can count on, looking very like the king, and a woman, looking very like the queen, as well as my son, who is the same age as the dauphin. You know how popular I am among the patriots; when they've seen me travel with these companions a couple of times, it will be easy to bring the royal family on a third trip. . . . Let me know if this proposition appeals to you; there is no time to be lost."

Of course the time was lost. She could not delay a second when Narbonne was denounced as a traitor to the nation; she hid him and a friend in the Swedish embassy. The sanctuary was invaded; Germaine was unruffled by her uninvited guests.

"I began," she told in her account of the Revolution, "by frightening these men to the best of my ability, by reminding them of the violation of international law of which they were guilty by entering the residence of an ambassador, and as they know next to nothing about geography, I persuaded them that Sweden, since her territory touched the French border, could attack France the next morning.

"The lower classes," she continued, "will swallow anything whole; there is nothing particularly refined about either their feelings or their ideas. With my heart in my mouth, I screwed up my courage and made a few jokes about the injustice of their suspicions."

Germaine was almost always equal to an emergency. She had the wit at this moment to call on Justus Erich Bollman, a German who made a career out of saving famous men from difficult situations—he was the one who set Lafayette (for a time) free from the prison of Olmütz. He promised to get Narbonne to England, and this he accomplished in four days.

But there was other work to be done, other friends to be saved. There was, for example, Lafayette's admirer Trophime-Gérard Marquis de Lally-Tollendal. Prison reform was a passion with Lally, but he was on the eve of knowing too much about the subject. He had been carted off to the Abbaye, and his execution was expected at any minute. Then there was Arnail-François Comte de Jaucourt, whose position was even more delicate. This dedicated Protestant, the proud founder of a society for biblical studies, could not, like Lally, talk himself out of almost any predicament.

In her anxiety Germaine turned to Pierre-Louis Manuel. This member of the Commune was an artisan's son, but Germaine recalled that he had once been a tutor in a banker's family. He was apparently an idealist. "You are no longer a king," he took the trouble to inform Louis XVI after August 10; "now you have the chance to become a good citizen." Manuel also had liter-

ary ambitions. He had just published a volume of Mira-
beau's letters. The preface was inadequate, but its very
existence allowed one to hope.

At seven in the morning Germaine made her appearance at Manuel's door. "That was a rather democratic
hour to meet anyone," she admitted. "But at least I was
on time. I arrived before he got up, I waited for him in
his office, and I noticed his own portrait on his desk.
That gave me hope that I could play upon his vanity.
He came in, and I must do him justice to say that I
won him over by appealing to his better nature."

In the end, after Condorcet and the British ambassador had pleaded for the life of Lally, he was set free,
and Manuel himself saw to it that Jaucourt was liber-
ated. A little more than a year later this generous member of the Commune was guillotined: he was so foolish
as to protest the execution of Louis XVI.

With Narbonne in England and Lally and Jaucourt
at liberty, Germaine could at last think of her departure
from Paris. She was leaving at an appropriate time. As
yet no woman had been murdered by the mob, but on
the very next day the head of the Princesse de Lamballe
was paraded on a pike beneath the windows of the
queen.

To begin to travel was to tremble, as Germaine discovered as soon as her carriage left the Swedish embassy. A horde of hags was waiting to claw her hair;
the mob was there to jeer that she was walking off with
all the gold of the nation. Her coachman was bullied
into driving her to the Assembly. There she found herself accused of plotting the escape of enemies of the
Revolution. She was ordered, at once, to the City Hall.

It took, she recalled, all of three hours for her to
make her way to the headquarters of the Commune.
She had to fend off huge crowds, and to listen, she
said, to her death sentence intoned by a thousand voices.

Not that anyone insulted her; she went unrecognized by the multitude. But her great carriage and the lace of her dress spelled a victim.

"Having no idea of how inhuman men become in a revolution," she wrote, "I called out two or three times to the gendarmes who came close to my carriage, and asked for help, but all they did was to threaten me. I was pregnant, but that did me no good at all; on the contrary, they became all the more irritable because they knew they were guilty. However, the gendarme they had placed beside me, being beyond their control, was moved by my plight, and he promised to defend me to the end."

He kept his word. When the time came for Germaine to climb the staircase of the City Hall, a guardsman aimed a spear at her which would have knocked her senseless, if the gendarme had not parried the blow with his sword. "If I had been knocked down," she reflected, "that would have been the last of me, for the common people have a certain respect for a person who is still standing, but once the victim has been thrown to the ground, that's the end."

For a second Germaine was happy that she had escaped the mob; then she realized that she would soon be face to face with Robespierre himself. She was not relieved when she listened to the representative of Parma, who had been arrested that morning. He refused to recognize her, and insisted that her case had nothing to do with his. "The poor man's lack of chivalry displeased me," she admitted, "and I became all the more anxious to defend myself, since it seemed that he had no desire to save me the trouble. So I got up and made plain my right to leave the city, as the wife of the Swedish ambassador, and I held out the passport that had been given me in recognition of my rights."

At that very moment Manuel appeared. Taking her

and her chambermaid in his custody, he led the way to his office to await the verdict. For six hours she paced the floor, dying, she wrote, of hunger, thirst, and fear. The window looked out on the Place de Grève, and she was watching the mob in the act of looting her carriage when suddenly a giant in the uniform of the National Guard leaped onto the coachman's seat and kept the populace at bay. She identified her friend as Santerre, a wealthy brewer with a weakness for the race tracks. But not so long ago he had been one of those in the Faubourg Saint-Antoine who distributed the wheat Necker made a point of handing out to the poor in hard times, and this was his way of showing his respect. He might, Germaine bitterly reflected, have done more; he might have come at once to her rescue.

At long last, after dark, Manuel sat beside her as she drove back to the Swedish embassy—it would not have been wise to join her in broad daylight. No street lamps were lit that night, but the torches held by the revolutionaries patrolling the streets were more terrifying than darkness itself. Manuel was stopped again and again; again and again he announced that he was the public prosecutor of the Commune, and they went on their way unmolested.

Once at the Swedish embassy Manuel explained that a new passport was on its way, and that a gendarme would accompany her and her maid—no one else was to be allowed in her carriage—to the Swiss frontier. The next morning Jean-Lambert Tallien knocked at her door; he had been detailed, he said, to see her beyond the gates of Paris. He had yet to prove himself— in the following year he would terrorize the great city of Bordeaux—but he was already an ominous radical. He could not avoid recognizing in her drawing room a number of her friends who could not be considered unqualified admirers of the Commune. Germaine was for some reason undiscouraged; she got him to promise that he would not reveal their names, and for some reason he kept his word.

"I got into the carriage with him," Germaine wrote, "and we said good-by without having said a word about what was on our minds. This was a time when words froze on one's lips."

She was with her father and her mother at Coppet by the 7th of September, but her heart was in England. "Here I am," she wrote Narbonne, "and I don't find the letter you promised. I implore you to write at least twice a week, using my Paris address." On the next day she was telling him that Auguste was an interesting child, but "already I feel stirring in my womb a new proof of our love."

By the middle of September she was reminding Narbonne that there was something about him that made him forget anyone who was far away. What if she died in childbirth? "Take care," she warned, "that I have nothing to reproach you for when I'm in labor. . . . Forgive me for being melancholy, but as I've often told you, all I want from you in exchange for my life is a sign of affection, and since I've only asked for a rose— a rose on which my life depends—I think it's cruel of you to refuse. . . . In ten weeks from now," she added, "another child born into this gloomy world will bring us even closer together."

She was hard at work on her treatise *On the Influence of Passion on Happiness*, but she was not so busy that she failed to consider what might happen if Staël showed up the moment the baby arrived. Supposing he called Auguste *his* son in her presence? Her blood boiled at the idea, even though her father pointed out that there might be many advantages to a reconciliation.

By the middle of October she confessed that her father had become tiresome. "He keeps on making insulting remarks about my pregnancy and my passion for you," she reported to Narbonne. In the meantime her mother, Bible in hand, was accusing Necker of being too kind to his erring daughter.

"What an awful institution marriage is!" she complained. "Monsieur de Staël, who still says he is in love with me, has just written my father a letter worthy of a monk with a wife on his hands." Would it be embarrassing to get a Swedish divorce, she wondered.

"I kneel down before your portrait," she wrote Narbonne on the 18th of November, "begging for the blessings which devout women find in religion." Forty-eight hours later she was delivered of her second son, Albert. He was "a pretty baby who, like his mother, will live only to love you, and to be another link between our inseparable fate."

Soon afterward Germaine heard that Narbonne was thinking of returning to France to defend his king. "The second you set foot in France," she threatened, "I'll blow my brains out. . . . I thought that my life meant more to you than this, the most mad, the most useless and most dangerous step either for you or the king. . . . If you leave England, I know what has to be done, and if you want me to kill myself, I'll do it."

Narbonne *must* come to Coppet. On Christmas day she was writing that if he knocked on her door, Necker promised to overlook their irregular relationship. The day after Christmas she reported that even her mother would condescend to receive her lover. "That's saying a great deal for her," she boasted. Two days later Germaine was in Geneva. "What I had to suffer in my father's house was so horrible that I fled here to get a breath of air." By then her mind was made up. She must go to Narbonne in England.

It was on the 20th of January, 1793, just twenty-four hours before Louis XVI was decapitated, that Germaine arrived at Juniper Hall at Mickleham in Surrey. Here she found Talleyrand, Jaucourt, Mathieu de Montmorency, and Narbonne himself. And here she met Fanny Burney, the dainty, undaring creator of *Evelina*.

"There can be nothing imagined more charming, more fascinating than this colony," Fanny wrote her father. "Between their sufferings and their *agrémens*, they occupy us almost wholly. Monsieur de Narbonne has no thousand pounds a year! he got only £4,000 at the beginning, from a most splendid fortune, and little foreseeing how all this has turned out, he has lived, we fear, upon the principal. . . . He bears the highest character for goodness, parts, sweetness of manners, and ready wit. You could not keep your heart from him if you saw him only for half an hour."

As for Madame de Staël, Fanny went on, "she is a woman of the first abilities, I think, I have ever seen; she is more in the style of Mrs. Thrale than of any other celebrated character, but she has infinitely more depth, and seems an even profound politician and metaphysician. She has suffered us to hear some of her works in ms., which are truly wonderful, for powers both of thinking and expression. She adores her father, but is much alarmed at having had no news from him since she has heard of the massacre of the martyred Louis. . . .

"Ever since her arrival she has been pressing me to spend some time with her before I return to town. She wanted Susan and me to pass a month with her, but, finding that impossible, she bestowed all her entreaties upon me alone, and they are so urgent . . . that she not only insisted upon my writing to you . . . but declares she will also write herself, to ask your permission for the visit. She exactly resembles Mrs. Thrale in the ardor and warmth of her temper and partialities. I find her impossible to resist, and therefore, if your answer to her is such as I conclude it must be, I shall wait upon her for a week. She is only a short walk from here. . . ."

Germaine was indeed anxious for a long visit with Fanny; she had written her in English. "When I learned to write English I began by Milton," she addressed the good doctor's daughter, "to know all or renounce all in once. I follow the same system in writing my first English letter to Miss Burney; after such an enterprise, nothing can affright me. I feel for her so tender a friendship that it melts my admiration, inspires my heart with hope of her indulgence, and impresses me with the idea that in a tongue even so unknown I could express sentiments so deeply felt."

Perhaps because Talleyrand had just criticized the manner in which she read her prose out loud, Germaine failed to reckon, as she should have, with the rumors reaching Dr. Burney of the life that was led at Juniper Hall. The doctor had already heard that his daughter "was in the habit of intimacy and much seeing the blasted character, Madame de Staël . . . who is in repute of wicked democratic esteem, and ran adulterously after a Monsieur de Narbonne."

"I am not at all surprised at your account of the captivating powers of Madame de Staël," wrote Dr. Burney to Fanny. "It corresponds with all I had heard about her, and with the opinion I formed of her intellectual and literary powers, in reading her charming little *Apologie de Rousseau*. But as nothing human is allowed to be perfect, she has not escaped censure."

Dr. Burney went on to the painful conclusion. "Her house," he told his daughter, "was the center of revolutionists previous to the tenth of August, after her father's departure, and she has been accused of partiality to Monsieur de N——." This, he conceded, could all be Jacobinical malignity. "However, unfavorable stories of her have been brought hither, and the Burkes . . . have repeated them to me. . . . I know this will make you feel uncomfortable, but it seemed right to me to hint it to you. If you are not absolutely in the house of Madame de Staël when this arrives, it would perhaps be possible for you to waive the visit to her by a compromise . . . and so make the addendum to your stay under her roof."

As a dutiful daughter, Fanny obeyed her father's injunction. She had, however, fallen in love with a certain Alexandre d'Arblay, an artillery officer who had joined Germaine's friends at Juniper Hall, and in the spring of 1793 she married him.

Germaine was aware of all of this. "Poor Madame de Staël has been greatly disappointed and hurt by the failure of the friendship and intercourse she wished to maintain with you," Fanny's sister Susan wrote her on the 14th of May.

Six days later Germaine was at Dover, the first stop on the long journey back to Coppet. She left Narbonne behind her; he had not, it seems, been found worth the voyage.

CHAPTER FOUR

THE TEMPTATIONS
OF A TRIO

———◆———

By staying in England Narbonne proved that he was unwilling to play the role of an ideal man. But he remained useful; to him Germaine could divulge the discontent she suffered as she journeyed back to Coppet and her children. "I speak only English nowadays, I worship England, I don't see how I ever said a word against that country," she wrote on her arrival in Cologne. "The Rhine reminded me of the Thames, and I broke into tears."

From Frankfurt she passed on the latest news of her husband. "I'm more disgusted with Monsieur de Staël than ever, and here's the reason. You may or may not know that I only made up to him in order to have a little more money. Now I learn that he's over his heels in debt. Added to all his other faults, he has a love of luxury you can't imagine. It isn't his generosity that has led him into debt, but showing off and pampering himself. He must bring his own bed along when he travels, the very best of horses, a pack of dogs, and three valets, and he thinks he is as democratic as Robespierre!

Nothing really is beneath him, for there is nothing more despicable than leading a life of luxury when everyone you know is terribly hard up, and luxury is really good for nothing. Nothing could make me more indignant than seeing you on foot while Monsieur de Staël goes riding in his carriage. . . . He must become a new man or we'll separate, for all I want out of him is a little more money, and I'd rather go begging than take advantage of any fortune you couldn't share."

By the time she reached Basel she expected the very worst from the coalition between her mother and her husband, and her temper was not improved by the sore throat she acquired at Coppet. "Monsieur de Staël," she reported, "was more than kind, but he'll never understand that pouring me a glass of lemonade will never give him your place in my heart." The more considerately her husband behaved, the more desperate she became. "He couldn't be more attentive," she confessed. "If he can stand seeing you as easily as he can stand talking about you, he'll be an angel, but that does not make his conversation any more bearable. I love him with all the power of my mind. . . . My mother is worse than ever."

But the duet she had been playing with Narbonne was not the only music she could conceive of. The temptations of a trio were evident when she wrote her lover in England on the 23rd of July that she had just met Adolphe Comte de Ribbing, a Swedish nobleman who had been unmistakably involved in the successful plot to murder Staël's patron, Gustavus III. The unfortunate king, who had been doing his best to check the spread of the French Revolution, was assassinated by aristocrats far to the right of his own political beliefs. Germaine might have paused before cultivating a reactionary like Ribbing, but then he was handsome, he was only twenty-eight, and his French was flawless. At the age of ten, he had taken the part of Joas in a performance of Racine's *Athalie*.

"We can't receive him," she complained to Narbonne. "But using one pretext or another, he has managed to meet us when we were out walking. He is terribly handsome to any woman with an eye for beauty. He is more of a tease than a good talker, but I can see he is yearning to fall in love with me. However, as long as M. de St. is around, my position as the ambassador's wife makes it impossible for me to see him. Seriously, is there any man in the world who would dare to make love to your mistress?"

Germaine did not mention one of Ribbing's charms. He had been sentenced to death for his part in the conspiracy, and set free only to be sent into exile.

By November she decided that she could not overlook this homeless wanderer. "For some time," she wrote Ribbing, "I have been thinking that you must have suffered all the remorse that anyone would need to form a strong character. This is a subject we must talk about in the long winter evenings ahead of us, and then I'll recite that line I quoted:

He believed he was less guilty when someone loved him.

Already in September Germaine was exasperated by Narbonne's lingering in England. "I must have a prompt and unequivocal answer," she warned him. "All I want is the words *I want* or *I don't want to come*. Anything else would be a lie, and I blush for you. If you don't want to come, I'll leave Monsieur de Staël and I'll go to London. That would be an infamous thing to do, but I see no alternative. It wouldn't do either one of us any good, for you would despise me, and I would end up hating you in your own treacherous and self-centered style. But you have dragged me, step by step, to the abyss. I can't have any respect for you, but then

I can't stop worshipping you. I can see that you don't need me, and I'll die if I don't see you again. Well, the sacrifice shall be consummated. After having made me a vile thing in my own eyes, you'll enjoy the last seconds of my life, and you'll survive the unhappy woman whom you have led astray. . . . On my knees I beg you to come by way of Holland under an assumed name. You can't say no to me!"

On the next day she disclosed that she fainted in the middle of a letter to Narbonne. "They went to fetch Monsieur de Staël," she wrote, "and when I regained consciousness, this is what he said: *I see very clearly, my dear, that Monsieur de Narbonne does not want to come to see you. For some time your father and I have foreseen that at the last minute he'd invent some pretext or other, and since he won't give in to you, it's plain that either he wants you to give up the idea of seeing him, or he wants you to go and find him yourself. You may worry yourself into the grave over all this, and since I can't make you happy, the least I can do is not to cause your death. Go and tell Monsieur de Narbonne that if he keeps on making all those miserable excuses —unworthy of both of you—that in a month, as soon as you receive a reply to your letter, I'll take you myself to Frankfurt, and from there you can get to England.*

"If you aren't here in a month's time," Germaine added, "I'll leave. . . . In the name of mercy, in the name of humanity, you must either come or send me some poison that will free me from you and from myself. . . . The lake is always there: why don't I throw myself into it instead of begging for mercy from a merciless man like you?"

Still no answer came, and by the middle of October she was again challenging her lover. "I should be happy to die this minute," she wrote, "for I now know that you are the most faithless and treacherous of men."

From Talleyrand she had heard that Narbonne had no intention of leaving England. "Before God," she went on, "I swear that if the reply to this letter isn't that you are on your way to Holland under the name of Lara, this is the last anyone will hear from the mother of your children, from the woman who saved your life, and from the woman whose life you should defend at any price, but whom you are slowly murdering."

She refused, however, to abandon all hope. "My whole life has been sacrificed to you since I was twenty-one," she wrote early in November, taking a year off her age as was her custom when communicating with Narbonne.

"Don't invent some new torture for me," she was writing late in January, 1794. "Wait for me in England, and let's merely be good friends. You won't have to explain your ingratitude, and I won't have to prove that you aren't simply a lover who has left his mistress, but a man who has cast out of his mind the most sacred ties that can unite two unhappy human beings."

"Sometimes," she was confessing a few days later, "I think that it is the very shamelessness of your conduct that makes it impossible for you to make amends. . . . You are the father of my children, my life has been thrown at your feet, everyone knows that I love you, you have meant so much to me that as soon as I see you again, I'll help you to deceive me, and I need your love so much that I'll be as grateful as if I had deserved nothing."

By the end of February she was once more threatening suicide. "There is some mystery, some enigma, some secret I can't explain about your conduct. . . . You have no good reason to insult a woman whose only fault in all her life is that she loved you. You are degrading yourself by showing such offensive disdain for the object of your love for five long years. . . . Can you possibly be anxious for Europe to ring with the news that Madame de Staël—the woman who has been all that I have been for you—has thrown herself into the lake because Monsieur de Narbonne stopped giving any sign of life, stopped at the very moment when he knew she was unhappy and could no longer offer him the same opportunities? . . . Go and find Bollman and ask him how I made up his mind to save your life. Think back to the 2nd of September, and remember that when they were about to butcher me, they kept yelling: *You saved Narbonne!* If only I had died at that very moment: to lose my life for you would have been glorious compared to the suicide to which I am brought nearer every day."

"I know I've lost you," she wrote early in March. "Poor Ribbing thought I was near death, and in spite of his extraordinary passion for me, was hoping you'd come, thinking it might be the only way to save me."

By the middle of March she was in Lausanne. Her mother was wasting away with dropsy. Germaine's only consolation was Ribbing. "He has become one of us," she bravely reported. "How often I've talked to him about you! How devoted I've been to you, and this at a time when his love would have driven any other woman wild. . . . He knows how to love me, he is a man of character, he's as forceful as he is sensitive. But if you love me still, don't be jealous. In all the world I have only you, my children, five years of memories, and your charm, which makes me forgive all. I could not spend a quarter of an hour with you without falling at your feet."

"My mother almost died last night, her breathing has become so painful," she wrote a week later. "She sent for me. She said: *My daughter, I am dying of the grief which your guilty and well-publicized love affair has caused me. You are punished by the conduct of your*

41

lover, which will put an end to the attachment which my prayers were powerless to break up. There is only one thing in the world that will bring my forgiveness in heaven, and that is the care you take of your father. Don't say a word to me. Get out! I can't possibly argue with you at this time.

"I left her," Germaine continued, "and I am sure I can stand anything, because I did not die then and there. . . .

"Speaking of Monsieur de Ribbing, you tell me that I'm a puzzling creature. No, I have not been flirting with him, but I would have liked to, I would like to have given him my heart, this heart that you have tossed aside, this heart that needs so much to be loved, this heart that can't stand being alone, this heart that can't live on trifles, the way yours can, this heart that you have torn apart with a cruelty that no tyrant could conceive of. *You say you need me more than I need you.* How vicious can you be?"

"It is true," she added three days later, "that in the year since I left you, you haven't once pronounced the names of my children. You must be ashamed to be their father. And how about me? What about my feelings when I look at them? . . .

"You bring up what I said about Monsieur de Ribbing," Germaine went on. "I am now ready to give myself to him. It was wrong of me to let him love me so passionately, without once welcoming, from the depths of the despair of that courageous soul, the outburst that would relieve me for a second from the awful weight on my heart. If I believe that this incredibly handsome man could have any effect on my senses, that I could experience five minutes of ecstasy by throwing myself at him, I would do it this very evening. Time after time I've approached him, as though it were my duty. I've told him: *I'll love you, I believe I could.* Then he has thrown himself at my feet, he has been eager to take me in his arms, but then a deathlike chill has come over me, and I've told him passionately again and again that you were the only person in the world who had a right to my heart. At the end of one of these scenes he was unconscious for half an hour in my grief-stricken house, and I forced him to go away, at least for a time. He is too fine a man, he is too kind, to let him hope for any reward from my sad life."

From Zurich in the middle of April she wrote Narbonne that "common sense and love could never mix. You would have been here a long time ago if I'd stopped writing you, and if you had heard from someone else that Monsieur de Ribbing has fallen wildly in love with me. I have given you an inkling of the truth. . . ."

Before April was over Germaine surrendered. "Now I know that my life is yours," she wrote Ribbing from Berne. "When I saw you leave, the blood rushed from my heart, and morally and physically I knew that we were one. Yes, I love you, and you can't have any doubts about that; there has been a struggle, but you have triumphed, and now I am in the conqueror's chariot. We have changed roles, but treat me with kindness now that I am your slave."

The trio had come to an end. Germaine was counting on the delights of the new duet when she wrote one of her last letters to Narbonne. "Apparently," she told him, "everything I believed I meant to you was a dream, and only my letters are real."

But she could not forget her father, not even in the arms of Ribbing. She hurried back to be with her father during her mother's last hours. Once, when there were no musicians in the house, Necker sent her to the piano, and she sang a sad air of Sacchini, Oedipus recalling the loving care of Antigone. This was more than her father could bear, and he broke into sobs at her mother's feet.

Madame Necker died on the 14th of May, and Germaine was there when her father's thoughts turned to the Alps beyond her window. The banker pointed to a cloud. "Perhaps her soul is floating here," he said.

Germaine's mother was carefully embalmed in a black marble tub filled with brandy; this was then laid in a small mausoleum at Coppet, with the understanding that her husband's body would one day lie beside hers for eternity. Her daughter realized that even in death she would be uttering precise comments on the nature of the perils of enthusiasm. "My father," she dutifully reported to the Baron de Staël, "is as superstitious about my mother's tomb as she herself in her lifetime."

But Suzanne Necker could not dictate her daughter's future. The dead woman could not raise a finger on the 18th of September, 1794, when Germaine came across, in a friend's drawing room at Lausanne, a young Swiss who was not yet twenty-seven—a year and a half younger than herself. He was lanky, his face was freckled, his red hair was curly, and he wore green glasses to protect his weak eyes. "I met this evening a very clever man whose name is Benjamin Constant," Germaine informed Ribbing. "He isn't very handsome, but he is terribly clever."

CHAPTER FIVE

HER BENJAMIN

———————————◆———————————

BENJAMIN CONSTANT was a passionate man who learned to analyze his own motives with the coolness of a chemist contemplating a formula. He wrote, but he has remained an author's author: the accuracy of his mind has always embarrassed the inaccurate public. To Germaine he was fatally attractive. Incredibly generous and intolerably honest, he taught her that passion spent was passion wasted unless every impulse was immediately and relentlessly exposed.

"There is," Benjamin observed, "something sacred about a suffering heart." He suffered much; he was not intended for happiness. Dissecting his own mind in his autobiographical novel *Adolphe*, he cursed any lover who doubted his love affair would last forever. Benjamin was born to doubt; he was also born to pity any woman who trusted his affection. "We are never corrupted by our senses," he believed. "We are corrupted by the calculations of the society we live in, and by the after-thoughts that experience engenders."

He was born at Lausanne on the 25th of October,

1767. His mother died the week after. His father, Juste Constant de Rebecque, a colonel in a Swiss regiment serving in the Netherlands, may have tried to guide his son, but he preferred taunting to teaching. "My father never censured me," Benjamin explained. "He was a cold and caustic observer who would begin almost any conversation by smiling indulgently, and then hurry off to another engagement." Juste Constant carried on more than one love affair. "It does them so little harm," he commented. "And it gives us so much pleasure."

Juste took a certain interest in Jeanne-Susanne Magnin, a girl whom he adopted when she was nine, and whom he made his mistress and possibly his wife. With Benjamin's mother dead, his first thought was that Jeanne-Susanne—or Marianne, as she was called—would make a perfect governess for the child. Juste's own mother disagreed; for the first five years of Benjamin's life she watched over him.

But in 1772, when Marianne turned twenty, she was shipped from Holland to Lausanne to look after Benjamin. She could not have been a perfect stepmother, and she was understandably anxious for children of her own. She bore Juste a son and a daughter whose precise relationship was a question that troubled Benjamin for some time. Perhaps the only consolation of Benjamin's childhood was the companionship of his cousin Rosalie. This nearsighted cripple (she had tripped from a hayloft ladder when a little girl) composed careful water colors of Alpine flowers and some of the most affectionate letters that Benjamin ever received.

Benjamin was only five when his father decided he might learn Greek. An odd German by the name of Stroelin was hired for the purpose; he succeeded quite well, for he persuaded his pupil that Greek was a secret language invented by both of them. But Stroelin was fond of beating the little boy; then he would hug him and make him promise not to tell his father. In the end Stroelin was found out and sent away, just when the elements of Greek grammar were fixed in the little boy's mind.

When Benjamin was seven, his father carried him to Brussels with the idea he would himself take charge of his son's education. He soon gave up the notion, and thought he had found an ideal tutor in Monsieur de la Grange, a Frenchman who had been the surgeon of his regiment. According to his pupil, Monsieur de la Grange was an atheist with a mediocre mind. He had a weakness for young girls, and he tried (whether he was successful, we do not know) to get into bed with the daughter of his charge's music teacher. He then took Benjamin to live in a brothel, so that his pleasures might be unsupervised. Here he was found by his scholar's father, and discharged.

For a time Benjamin went to live with the family of his music master. There he came upon a lending library, and devoured so many volumes of atheistic and pornographic literature that his eyesight was permanently damaged. He was nine when he was entrusted to a Monsieur Gobert, a lawyer who had fled from France under peculiar circumstances, and was now anxious to set up a school with his mistress as principal. Monsieur Gobert was an amateur historian; he forced his pupil to make a number of copies of a manuscript he was preparing for the printers, and incidentally he taught him a little Latin. In the meantime Monsieur Gobert and his mistress had become the talk of the town; once again Benjamin was carried off by his father.

Juste's next choice as a tutor was a Monsieur Duplessis, an unfrocked monk who had gone into hiding in the neighborhood of Neuchâtel. He was a kind man but a weakling. He did his best to educate Benjamin for more than a year, taking him from Switzerland to Belgium and then to Holland. He was, however, something of a bore in Juste's opinion, and he too was let go. Later he became a tutor to the young Comte D'Aumale. Forgetting that he was in his fifties, he fell in love with young D'Aumale's sister and blew his brains out when a wigmaker took his place in her bed.

Benjamin was now thirteen years old, and his father thought it was time he went up to Oxford. Once they arrived in England, Juste discovered that almost no one entered the university before the age of twenty. For a month or two he stayed on, teaching English to his son and amusing himself elsewhere. He then hired a Mr. May, an Englishman whom he considered to be a ridiculous fellow and whom he did not hesitate to sneer at in his son's presence. But for a year and a half Mr. May followed the Constants across the Continent, never once gaining his pupil's confidence. A Monsieur Bridel, who was engaged in Switzerland when Mr. May was sent back to England, proved to be even more of a mistake. He was, Juste decided, an unforgivably pretentious pedant.

Benjamin was not quite fifteen when his father declared that only a German university would do. For some reason Erlangen was selected, possibly because it was in the neighborhood of the court of Bayreuth. "I must have been quite entertaining," Benjamin recollected. He said everything he had on his mind to the old Margravine, who instantly took him up. However, he had to have at least the reputation of keeping a mistress, and he was so indiscreet as to choose a girl whose reputation was unfortunate and whose mother had been particularly impertinent to the Margravine. "The strange thing," he put down in his red notebook, "is that, on the one hand, I was far from being in love with the girl, and that, on the other hand, we never slept to-

48

gether. Very likely I am the only man she ever resisted. But the pleasure of letting everyone know, and of hearing everyone say that I was keeping a mistress more than made up, both for spending my time with a person I was not at all in love with, and for not taking advantage of the woman I was keeping."

Of course the Margravine was highly incensed, and the behavior of the mother of Benjamin's make-believe mistress did not improve matters. When Juste sent for his son, who had been forbidden to show his face at court, he found that Benjamin had run up a considerable debt playing faro with the Margrave. Juste cheerfully paid off the Margrave, and entered his son, who was not yet sixteen, at the University of Edinburgh.

At Edinburgh Benjamin saw that it was fashionable to study, and he did, impressing a number of serious-minded young men, one of whom ended a distinguished career by presiding over the courts of Bombay. But his best friend was one John Wilde, a tobacconist's son; apparently as sensible as he was brilliant, nevertheless Wilde went insane not long after publishing a book that might have established his reputation. In the meantime Benjamin went gloriously into debt to the faro bank kept by the brother of his Italian music master.

At the end of his year and a half in Scotland Benjamin set off for Paris to meet his father. He promised his creditors he would make good; whether the debts were ever paid is another question. In Paris a certain Monsieur Suard agreed to introduce him into the best society. But as no room was immediately available at Suard's house, Benjamin took lodgings elsewhere. This meant that he was exposed to the company of a rich and very dissolute Englishman, whose manner of life he copied so carefully that he contracted debts he had no hope whatever of paying. When he finally got his room at Suard's, his father was bound to consult the Protestant chaplain of the Dutch ambassador. The chaplain turned Benjamin over to the care of a Monsieur Baumier. Ostensibly a Protestant who had been hounded by his family for his religious convictions, Baumier was perhaps the most depraved of all the men that Juste trusted. He was also an insolent bore, and when he began complaining of his charge's conduct, there was nothing to do but see what arrangements could be made in Brussels.

At eighteen in Brussels Benjamin fell in love with a Madame Johannot, a woman of twenty-eight who told him that she loved him. For this experience he was eternally grateful, and he could never think of her in later life without the most exquisite regret. Her husband, whose morals were deplorable, was one of the bullies who urged the execution of Louis XVI. He forced his wife to live in the same house with his mistress; sickened by his vices and by the presence of the other woman, Madame Johannot killed herself.

While recovering in Switzerland from his infatuation, Benjamin laid the foundations for a major work he did not live long enough to see through the press. This was a history of religions, the notes for which he sketched on the back of tarot cards. "At that time," he confessed, "I did not have the necessary information to write four sentences on such a subject. Brought up on the principles of the eighteenth century and particularly on those of Helvetius, my only thought was to do my share in destroying what I called prejudices."

From all this he was momentarily distracted by a woman in her thirties, Mrs. Trevor, the wife of the British ambassador to Turin. "She had been very beautiful," he recalled, "and she still had pretty eyes, superb teeth, and a charming smile." He wrote her a passionate love letter, and when she replied by offering her friendship, he was obliged to advertise his despair by rolling on the ground and dashing his head against the walls of the drawing room. Nothing further happened. "I was excessively timid and frantically eager; I did not yet understand that we must take without asking; I was always asking and never taking."

With that Benjamin went on to Paris where he found a certain satisfaction playing cards with an old French-woman to whom he had been introduced by Mrs. Trevor. His new friend gambled in her carriage, gambled in bed, gambled in her bath, morning, noon, and night. And he lost not only every penny his father could give him, but every penny he could borrow.

On one of the many occasions on which his credit was exhausted, Benjamin thought of calling on Madame Saurin, a woman of sixty-five who had been kind to him, and whom he had often made fun of. "You may well be astonished," he told her, "by the step I have taken. I am awfully sorry if you have an unfavorable impression of me." He paused to ask if she had received a letter from him; she had not. "You've been so kind to me," he went on, "you have shown so much interest in what I was doing! Perhaps I have been too presumptuous. But there are times when a man loses his head. I could never forgive myself if I had done anything to lose your friend-ship. Please, put that unfortunate letter out of your mind. Let me conceal from you something that slipped out in a moment of great distress."

"How can you doubt my love for a second?" asked Madame Saurin. "I must know everything. Go on. Go on." She hid her head in her hands. She trembled from head to foot.

It was now evident to Benjamin that she had taken everything he had said for a declaration of love. "After all," he began again, "I don't see why I should bore you any longer with a trifling matter. I've been so fool-ish as to gamble at cards, I've lost a little more than I happen to have in the world, and I wrote to ask if you would have the kindness to lend me what I need to pay my debts."

For a second Madame Saurin was motionless. Then she removed her hands from her face, got up without saying a word, and paid exactly the sum he asked for.

It was about this time, when Benjamin was twenty, that he made the acquaintance in Paris of Madame de Charrière, a Dutchwoman of forty-seven. She had written novels, but her mind was so precise that he was pleased. "She was," we have his word for it, "the first intelligent woman I had met, and one of the most intelligent I have ever met."

She had been amused long ago by James Boswell's pretensions, she had put up with the bantering of one of Benjamin's uncles, and at thirty had married a shy Swiss who had been engaged to tutor her brother in conic sections. This meant that she was relegated for most of her life to a manor house near Neuchâtel, where her only company, aside from her inconspicuous husband, was his aged father and two spinster ladies of the family. She might be forgotten in the twentieth century, if Geoffrey Scott had not written that almost perfect biography *The Portrait of Zélide*.

Zélide—Madame de Charrière's maiden name was Isabelle van Seeroskerken van Tuyll, but she called herself Zélide when she came to do a self-portrait in prose—was an unusual woman. It may have been true, as Scott asserted, that "mathematics consoled her for the obscurity of religion." But was it equally true that her "eighteenth-century mind could not doubt for a moment that logic was the basis of human happiness"? Logical she may have been, to a point, but the second she welcomed Benjamin she was in the presence of a man who never hesitated to follow reasoning to the most unreasonable conclusions. She pitied him, she forgave him, and she may have earned a greater compliment than Scott bestowed.

"Her mind enchanted me," Benjamin wrote. "We talked for days and nights on end. She was a very severe critic of everyone she met. I was naturally caustic. We were a perfect match. . . . Madame de Charrière had such an original and lively way of looking at life, such scorn for prejudices, such a strong mind, and was so vigorously and disdainfully superior to the average person, that for me, queer and disdainful man that I was at twenty, her conversation was an enjoyment such as I had never known."

Zélide's husband, who was honestly grateful for her accomplishments, did his best to encourage her friendship for Benjamin, and all went smoothly until another woman took it into her head to warn Juste of what was going on. This informant took the trouble to point out that his son might marry Mademoiselle Pourrat, a girl sixteen years old of whom he had already seen something, and who had an income of 80,000 francs a year. This was an attractive idea to Benjamin's father, and he lost no time in writing that if he wanted to stay on in Paris, he must make this dream come true.

Benjamin, who could be an obedient son, at once wrote Mademoiselle Pourrat's mother to ask for her hand. The reply, which was gracefully phrased, made plain that she was already engaged to another. Whereupon Benjamin wrote her the most violent love letter imaginable. To this Mademoiselle Pourrat answered by reminding him that her fate was in her parents' hands. What was this but the opportunity to write still another love letter? He at once offered to run off with her. "One might have thought I was writing to a victim that had begged for my assistance," he noted, "to a person who was as passionately fond of me as I was of her; the fact was that all my romantic epistles were addressed to a very matter-of-fact girl who did not love me in the least, who was far from dissatisfied with the man they had chosen for her, and who had given me neither the opportunity nor the right to write her in that way. But I was far along, and I had no intention of giving up, no matter what happened."

Now and then Benjamin happened to meet Mademoiselle Pourrat. On these occasions he never breathed a word about his letters. As soon as he was alone with her, he became extremely shy. But he was talkative in the presence of her mother; he remembered that she had a lover, and once, when he was especially vehement, the lover appeared and expressed his concern. For Madame Pourrat there was only one way out of this difficulty. She took Benjamin by the hand, led him to her lover, and asked him to make a solemn pledge that he was in love, not with her but with her daughter. "I looked at this situation from another point of view," Benjamin explained. "I saw myself dragged before a stranger to confess that I was an unhappy lover, a man disdained by mother and daughter. My pride was injured; I became delirious."

It so happened that he had a flask of opium in his possession. Madame de Charrière had been indulging in opium to quiet her nerves. He could tell that Madame Pourrat's lover was about to ask a few questions; these would be humiliating—as a matter of fact, they would be intolerable. "I was sure," Benjamin has written, "that if I swallowed the opium, no questions would be asked. Besides, for a long time I had been positive that one way of pleasing a woman is to try to commit suicide for her.

"This idea is not exactly correct," he admitted. "If you have already made an impression on a woman, and she is waiting to fall into your arms, it may be wise to threaten her with your suicide, because then you are offering her an excuse which is not only perfect but quick and honorable. But if the woman is not in love with you, neither the threat nor the thing will have any effect whatsoever. There was a fundamental mistake in my escapade with Mademoiselle Pourrat: I was inventing a romance in which I was the only actor."

Benjamin swallowed the opium. There was not enough in the bottle to do much damage, and since Madame Pourrat's lover threw himself in the way, more than half of the bottle was spilled on the carpet. But everyone was frightened, and Benjamin was obliged to gulp down a fluid that tasted vile but was intended to counteract the opium's effects. "I did everything I was asked to do," Benjamin confessed. "They might have made a fuss, and that would have been boring." He even listened to a short sermon on his misconduct.

Finally, after the antidotes had been administered, and Benjamin appeared to be none the worse, Mademoiselle Pourrat entered the room. She was on her way to the Opera, where Beaumarchais' *Tarare* was being given its first performance. Madame Pourrat suggested that he might escort her daughter for the evening, and he accepted.

Madame Pourrat was more reflective the next morning. On reading Benjamin's letters to her daughter, she decided that he would no longer be welcome to her house. She sent for Monsieur de Charrière; then sent for her daughter, and she had the satisfaction of hearing her daughter inform Monsieur de Charrière that Benjamin had never made love to her and that she was, moreover, very happy with her parents' choice. With this explanation Monsieur de Charrière announced that he was satisfied. Later on he told Benjamin that if Mademoiselle Pourrat had shown the slightest interest in him, he would have tried to convince her mother that the would-be suicide was the perfect suitor.

Benjamin was not really disappointed by his failure to conquer an heiress. Zélide was there to console him. "All of the convictions held by Madame de Charrière were based on her scorn for what was approved in the best society," he later realized. "We outdid each other in making fun of everyone we met: we got drunk on our own jokes and our scorn for mankind, with the result that I behaved in the fashion I've just described, occasionally laughing like a madman for a half an hour at something I'd done in dead earnestness half an hour before when I was deep in despair. . . . Madame de Charrière . . . was the only person with whom I could talk freely, because she was the only one who didn't bore me giving advice and making scenes about my conduct."

This was probably true, but Juste de Constant saw no reason to indulge his son a day longer. He ordered a Monsieur Benay, a lieutenant in his regiment, to bring Benjamin to Holland at once. Whereupon Benjamin borrowed thirty louis from Madame de Charrière and went out to dinner at the Palais-Royal with his guardian. At the Palais-Royal they came across a chemist who knew his way in the finest gambling hells. Benjamin could not resist telling him that he was thinking of running away. "Where to?" "Why, England," came the answer. "A very fine country," the chemist remarked. "The English enjoy a certain freedom." And when, at the end of his own dinner, the chemist observed that Benjamin was still in the restaurant, he laughed at him. "What! You haven't left yet?"

This was a reproach that could not be borne.

Monsieur Benay and his charge no sooner climbed into the carriage that was to take them to Holland than the former complained he was most uncomfortable. (For once grumbling was heaven-sent.) "I made the most of his fussing," wrote Benjamin, "for the idea came to me that if we turned back, I'd once again have the liberty to do exactly what I pleased." Return to Paris they did, and after Benjamin had walked up and down the floor of his room for half an hour, his mind was made up. He pocketed his thirty louis, grabbed a shirt, and shot for the front door.

He spent the rest of the night with a woman of easy virtue who happened to be an old acquaintance, taking care to down enough champagne to chase the last bit of common sense out of his mind. The next morning he was off to Calais in a carriage of his own. From London he wrote his father that he was in dire need of solitude. He asked his permission to spend three months in absolute quiet, and he hinted he would like nothing better than to be married and bring his wife to live with the two of them.

"The truth was," Benjamin set down in his autobiographical notes, "that I had no idea what I was putting down on paper, but I had a real need to rest after six months of mental and physical worry, and finding myself absolutely alone and completely free for the first time in my life, was frightfully anxious to enjoy this opportunity, which I had dreamed of for so long."

How Benjamin borrowed from this friend or that, how he traveled from London to Brighton and up to Edinburgh, how often he was drunk, how easily he shocked a landlord by preferring tea to wine, or how he came upon a Latin scholar who spent three hours each morning combing his hair—all this would take time better devoted to his life on the Continent. Eventually he found his way back to his father in Holland.

"I was horribly depressed," Benjamin revealed in his diary, "and for some time didn't have the physical strength to find my father's lodgings. But I screwed up my courage and I went on my way. . . . I kept shuddering at the incriminations that could justly be leveled

57

at me, and I was even more worried by my father's grief, and by the state of his health under the burden of such grief. His very last letters had been heart-rending. He had written me that he was sick at heart over what I had done, and that if I stayed any longer, I might be responsible for his death. I went into his room. He was playing whist with three officers of his regiment."

"Oh, there you are," said Juste. "How was your trip?"

"I told him," Benjamin wrote, "that I had traveled day and night, half on horseback and half in carriage. He kept on playing cards. I was waiting for him to make a scene as soon as we were alone. Finally everyone left."

"You must be tired," said Juste. "Go to bed." He took him to his own room, and as they went down the hall, he noticed that his son's clothing was torn. "My worst fears have been realized," he said.

"I was," Benjamin confessed, "completely bewildered by this reception, which was neither what I had feared nor what I had hoped for. In spite of my fears of being treated with the severity I deserved, I had a real need, even if I were scolded, for a frank explanation with my father. I should have liked to have begged his forgiveness, and to have talked over my plans with him. I was anxious to regain his confidence, and mine in him. I hoped that, for all my misgivings, we might have a heart-to-heart talk the next morning."

However, nothing happened the next morning, nor the morning after. "I thought," Benjamin set down, "that I should have broken the ice. His silence horrified me; mine very likely hurt his feelings. He attributed my silence to my frivolity, blameworthy indeed in view of my inexcusable conduct. And what I took for indifference was perhaps only his resentment in secret.

But on this occasion, as on a thousand others in my life, I was paralyzed by a timidity that I was unable to outgrow, and my words died on my lips, as soon as I saw I was not encouraged to continue."

Sent off to Berne, Benjamin managed to spend forty-eight hours with Madame de Charrière at Neuchâtel. He then discovered that he was to be exiled to the court of Brunswick, where his father had found him an appointment as Gentleman of the Chamber to the Duke. He was not enchanted by his surroundings. "The Germans," he wrote Madame de Charrière early in 1788, "are heavy. Heavy when they try to reason, heavy when they try to make jokes, heavy when they are sentimental, heavy when they are having a good time, heavy when they are bored."

Later that year the young man of twenty-one came upon a young woman of thirty sitting on a sofa crying her eyes out. He asked the cause, and was told she was unloved. For Benjamin this was sufficient; they were immediately engaged, and on the 8th of May, 1789, he was married to Wilhelmina von Cramm, the daughter of a captain in the Brunswick army. Apparently she was undistinguished, apart from her passion for pets which she ultimately indulged by keeping 121 birds, two squirrels, six cats, eight dogs, and a number of magpies, crows, and fish, all of which were housed in a single but commodious room.

This could not be a lasting attachment; despite her pets Minna found another lover. A deed of separation between Benjamin and Minna was signed on the 30th of March, 1793; by the end of 1795 they were divorced. But as early as January, 1793, Benjamin had met in Brunswick Georgina Charlotte Augusta, Countess of Hardenberg, the wife of the Baron von Marenholz. Charlotte was a good and trusting woman, and if Benjamin had been intended for the role of husband, she would have made him a good wife. The passion that he spent on her, and the remorse he suffered when he reviewed his tantalizing moments of hesitation—something of this has been preserved in the glacial prose of the autobiographical novel *Adolphe*.

Ellénore, the heroine of this work, who was partly modeled on Charlotte, "did not have an exceptional mind; but she could think clearly, and the phrases she used, which were always straightforward, were sometimes striking, thanks to the nobility of her soul. She had a great many prejudices, but all of her prejudices were founded on what was against her own interest. She set the greatest importance on being proper, precisely because her own behavior was not proper in the usual sense of the word. She was extremely religious, for religion was bound to condemn the life she led."

For several months Benjamin and Charlotte lived together. Her husband raised no difficulties, but her father was anxious to cultivate his scruples, and he decided that she must return to her parents' home. Whether Benjamin was brave at this moment is an interesting question. He consented to be separated from Charlotte; his anguish was exquisite if we may believe the reproaches he leveled at himself in *Adolphe*.

In the meantime his father had been involved in a series of fantastic lawsuits, and he discovered, to his intense disappointment, that Madame de Charrière did not intend to believe that Juste was invariably in the right. "My father's conduct," he explained to Zélide, "in every one of his cases has been strictly in accordance with the law. In spite of all this I pray God that He will keep you in His heavenly care and I beg you earnestly to burn all my letters. I burnt yours before I left Switzerland."

Madame de Charrière was displeased by the tone of this. "Send me a note—signed in full—saying that you have burnt *all* my letters. I shall then at once burn yours," she wrote. This message she signed and sent to the post office. But she retrieved it, and in the summer of 1794, when he left Brunswick, having resigned his post at the court, he went straight to Switzerland and Zélide.

One of her new acquaintances was Germaine, who had been so generous as to express an interest in her novel *Mistress Henley*. That is, she went so far as to ask for the loan of a copy. "I haven't been able to find one in Geneva," she wrote late in the summer of 1793. "I must have something of yours at hand to persuade me that I haven't really left you. . . . It's in Holland, I believe, that the best French is spoken."

A month later Germaine was writing Zélide again. "If I am to enjoy all the charms of society, I must have you at my side. Let me know if you happen to hear of a good house for rent in your part of the world."

This was praise, but Madame de Charrière did not surrender. "I can," she said, "easily forgive Madame de Staël for being in tune with the times. As for me, I'm not. I can't make myself any younger than I am, and I despise her affectations." In the end she decided that Germaine was an artificial creation, invented by Abbé Raynal of the Necker circle, abetted by Monsieur Guibert and her mother and father. Without their help, Germaine might have been nothing at all. Again, she might have amounted to something. "It would be rather amusing," Zélide reflected, "to tell her to her face exactly what one thinks of her."

Carelessly, Zélide confided her impressions to Benjamin, sure that once he saw Germaine he would understand. "She is very far from being unpretentious, she doesn't always think clearly, and what passes for her temperament is really her intellect. But you may admire her when you see her."

And then, on the 18th of September, 1794, Benjamin met Germaine.

"I don't find it at all difficult to give her, as you would say, her due," he wrote Zélide three days later. "On the contrary, the more I see of her, the more difficult it becomes for me not to praise her extravagantly, so that everyone I meet will understand the extent of my fascination and my admiration. I have rarely seen anyone so charming, so brilliant, so wise, so good, so thoughtful, so fantastically generous, so poised in society, so natural when I am alone with her. *She is the second woman I've met for whom I would have given everything in the world, and who would have meant everything in the world to me. You know who was the first.*"

As if this were not sufficient, Benjamin wrote Zélide once more on the 30th of September. "My trip to Coppet," he reported, "came off rather well. Madame de Staël was not at home, but I caught up with her on the road, climbed into her carriage, and went on to Nyon with her, then breakfast, dinner, supper, and breakfast again, so that I've had a chance to see her and talk to her. It seems to me that you judge her somewhat severely. I think she's very energetic, very rash, very talkative, but very good, very trusting. She is no mere talking machine; the proof of that is the very real concern she displays for anyone she has known who is in trouble. . . .

"It's true, as you say, that she has her silly side; she is as much of a name-dropper as any *parvenue*, and she can't resist talking about Paris society like a girl from the country. But I don't think she's vain; she simply knows that she is very intelligent, and she has to talk, to let herself go, and forget about anything like restraint. She does overpraise people, but that's because she wants to make friends, and to be as free as possible with them. Once they're gone, she very naturally changes her mind. You can't call that being unfaithful."

Apparently it took some time for Madame Charrière to realize what had happened. "In my detachment from you," she wrote Benjamin a year and a half later, "there is just what's needed to make one of the most beautiful attachments conceivable."

For Madame de Charrière the 18th of September, 1794, was the end. For Benjamin Constant it was a beginning to which there could be no end.*

* In his diary (which may have been written after the event) Benjamin insisted he first met her on the 19th. But a recently published letter of Madame de Staël to Ribbing, dated September 18, 1794, makes it plain that the 18th is the correct date.

CHAPTER SIX

THE CENTER OF
THE STAGE

A L T H O U G H Germaine had come across Benjamin
in an Alpine setting, she did not intend to forgive the
Alps. "I am," she confessed, "horribly bored by everything Swiss. These great mountains," she went on, "shut
us off from the world as completely as convent gates.
We lead the most dreadfully peaceful existence. We
might as well be dead in this dreary waste." As for the
dead, they presented problems of their own, proving
that sentiment was a plant that thrived in the climate of
Geneva. Her mother had been so thoughtful as to order
a servant to place a fresh letter from her to her husband
every day atop her tomb. The supply was plentiful; the
correspondence continued for well over a year. Necker
may have been touched by this attention from beyond
the grave. Germaine may have been exasperated.

Perpetually unprepared for a permanent attachment,
she had found in Benjamin a man as passionate as herself—and just as ill adapted to a situation that might
resemble marriage. They loved each other dearly; they
loved even more the torments they inflicted on each

other. But neither could be content to go on playing a part on a stage that was far from Paris. To be exiled from the capital was unbearable; it was also unthinkable by the summer of 1794. On the 27th of July the Terror had come to an end; priests were no longer drowned in droves by the exacting adherents of Saint-Just and Robespierre; the time had come for Germaine to resume the political role for which she was so enthusiastically qualified.

For the moment, however, she compromised by leasing the Château de Mézery near Lausanne. Here Benjamin came to live with her. So did the Comte de Jaucourt (whom she had rescued from the guillotine) and the Comtesse. So did Mathieu de Montmorency and his mother the Comtesse de Laval. They too were in her debt, for she had used her influence on their behalf when the great names of France were threatened. This was a kindness that Madame de Laval repaid by claiming the Comte de Narbonne for her own. Now that Germaine's passion had cooled, he also made himself welcome in this Swiss replica of Juniper Hall.

Germaine could overlook this triumph of Mathieu's mother. She was aware of Benjamin's devotion. "It is really curious," he wrote about this time, "to see how grateful women can be for the silliest things that are done to please them. I had an understanding with Madame de Staël that, in order not to embarrass her, I shouldn't stay in her room after midnight. No matter how charming I found her conversation, no matter how eager I was to go beyond mere talk, I had to give in to her firm resolution. But one evening, when the time (so I thought) had flown faster than usual, I took out my watch to prove that the hour for my departure had not yet struck. The inexorable dial proved that I was wrong, and in a burst of childlike anger, I smashed the instrument of my disgrace on the floor. 'How silly can you be! You are absurd!' Madame de Staël cried out. But I could see that she was smiling to herself in spite of it all. Really, that broken watch did me a great favor." He added: "I haven't bought another; I haven't had to."

There came another midnight at Mézery when Benjamin, according to the other colonists, was feeling rather sorry for himself; all day he had been difficult. Suddenly the most horrible shrieks were heard coming from his apartment. The servants rushed to his room. There he was in bed, pale, haggard, writhing with convulsions that left no doubt he was delirious. The alarm was sounded. "Monsieur Constant is dying!" rang through the house. Madame Rilliet-Huber, an old friend and confidante of Germaine, was one of the first to arrive on the scene. "Ah, Madame," said Benjamin, fixing his visitor with an agonizing glance, "tell her that I am dying for her. Ask her, in the name of a dying man, to come and listen to a last farewell, if there is still time, so that I may die a happy man, having seen her."

"I'm coming," said Germaine to Madame Rilliet-Huber. "His life is at stake."

Mathieu de Montmorency, who had been reading Saint Augustine in his dressing gown, was not pleased to be interrupted. "Throw that man out of the window!" he cried. "He's done all he could to upset the whole house, and now he's disgracing the place with a suicide." But he snuffed out his candle and followed Germaine down the hall.

"What have you done!" Germaine sobbed the second she saw Benjamin.

"It's you, it's you!" he moaned. "The sight of you is enough to call me back to life."

"You must live, you must!" Germaine shrieked. "I implore you!"

"If that is your command," Benjamin answered, "I

shall try to live."

"Great gods! What a comedy!" murmured Mathieu de Mortmorency. By the time the doctor arrived, the miracle of Benjamin's resurrection had taken place.

"It's strange, isn't it, my dear," Germaine said to Madame Rilliet-Huber as they left the room, "the way Constant took me literally. You did tell me he was dying."

"Well," Madame Rilliet-Huber confessed, "that's what he told me, and you believed it when you saw him."

"He also told me that he would try to live, and I hope he'll keep his promise to me," Germaine observed.

"That would be only fair," said Germaine's friend.

"It would be polite of him, wouldn't it?" Germaine said. The two women laughed, and just then Germaine remembered that Benjamin had kissed her hand in his agony. While Madame Rilliet-Huber watched, she bathed her hand in Eau de Cologne.

"I can see you're washing your hands of him," said Germaine's friend.

"Oh, yes," Germaine agreed, "and my conscience is not in the least troubled." Later she told Madame Rilliet-Huber that "I know I have a physical antipathy for that man that I can never overcome."

This was not the truth. A month or so later Benjamin and Germaine signed a most solemn agreement. "We promise," the document reads, "to devote our lives to each other, we swear that we are bound to each other for life, that we can never be divided, that we will never contract any other attachment, and that we will strengthen the ties that bind us as soon as we are able to do so.

"I declare," Benjamin went on for his part, "that I make this pledge with all my heart and soul, that I can't imagine anything in the world more lovely than

67

Madame de Staël, that I have been the happiest of men during the four months I've spent with her, and that I know the greatest privilege of my life will consist of making her a happy woman in her youth, growing old with her in peace and quiet, and reaching the end of my days at the side of a woman who understands me, and without whom life on earth would be meaningless."

Germaine was not always as serious as this. One morning she noticed that her lover had taken the trouble to brush and comb his hair before entering her room. "Benjamin," she said, "I can tell that you no longer love me."

She was delighted by his adoration; she was also amused. "Monsieur Constant," she wrote Ribbing in the fall of 1794, "has fallen wildly in love with me; he makes one scene after another, and he's so terribly unhappy that he's lost the only charm he had—a very good mind. I have to pity him, and now and then I'm bored—that is, when I forget for a second that no one, not even my Adolphe, has ever loved me so deeply. If you hear that Monsieur Constant has gone and killed himself, don't think I'm to blame. . . . Completely oblivious of the fact that his physical appearance is an invincible obstacle—even for someone not in love with you—he has gone out of his head. He falls into a faint whenever he sees me rearranging your portrait, and the only alternative I have to sending him away is forcing him to listen to me talking about you."

Exactly what Germaine had in mind was revealed five days later. "Yesterday," she wrote Ribbing, "I was horribly depressed by the black mood of that Esau Constant. He thought he could catch me off my guard by making an awful scene, and he kept telling me, as if I didn't know it, that Monsieur de Narbonne is a perfect bore. At that moment I had an inspiration. I said, just as if you were in the room, and just as if I were offering my prayers to you: 'I love the most exceptional man on earth; if he doesn't find me unworthy of him, he may dispose of my life. My future belongs to him.' I won't bother you by giving you a description of the blast that followed. I left the room just after I'd said this, and I believe that dark and somber man won't enter my room for some time."

In the meantime Germaine had other worries. "Monsieur de Narbonne is really impossible," she informed Ribbing. "He has been trying to win me back, and he has found all the proof he needed that I was in love with no one but Adolphe."

By November Benjamin was writing her five letters a day. In December she told Ribbing that "Benjamin Constant is coming down with consumption. He's so passionately in love with me that I feel sorry for him; I do all I can to get him to go traveling. Yesterday he said something that was rather witty; every time I allow him to see me, he talks about you, and that's why I listen to him. Yesterday he asked for the answer I've given him a thousand times already. 'Are you really in love with Comte Ribbing?' I blushed and kept silence. 'Isn't silence in itself an answer?' he said. 'You convey the idea, but you deprive me of the sound of your voice.' That was charming. He has a very good mind, but he's not much to look at, especially since he's so painfully in love."

Early in January Germaine was having her troubles with Mathieu de Montmorency. She let Ribbing know that "Mathieu has read the message written on my heart and which can't be kept a secret from the world; he is aware of the extent of my love for you. . . . He was really broken up by this. Now that he knows he hasn't a chance, he is even more devout than when you last saw him. . . . He practices the Catholic Religion as though he were a priest. I do all I can to tear him away from this way of life, but his only answer is that a hopeless passion has forced him to take this step, and that this is the only way he can tolerate the decision I've taken to be forever yours."

By March Germaine had all she could stand of another lodger at Mézery. "Monsieur de Narbonne," she wrote Ribbing, "has become a slave to Madame de Laval, and this connection has renewed all the hatred that woman had for me; she has stirred him up and made him behave very badly; he has gone around everywhere saying that I was in love with you and wanted to marry you."

As for Benjamin, "he smashes his head on the fireplace whenever I ask him to leave the room. He'll drag me to Paris in spite of myself, *If you don't come to see me*. He's an awfully clever madman even if he is extremely unpleasant to look at, but he is a madman, and he for one reason and Monsieur de Narbonne for another would be enough to make me think twice before staying on in Switzerland with you."

"Do you really want me to say something about Benjamin?" she asked in another letter. "You've put in a good word for him, but you don't deserve any praise for that. He is really very intelligent in spite of all you've heard, and I must tell you there are very few other people I so much enjoy talking to, especially about literature. So much for his accomplishments. As far as his character is concerned, he has devoted himself to me, under the conditions I've laid down, more faithfully than anyone I could imagine. That's all. He has no personality and he has no looks, and I can't conceive of falling in love with a man lacking either one of those advantages."

Whether Ribbing was reassured by this last sentence is open to question. On the 15th of May, 1795, Germaine set off for Paris with Benjamin at her side. The

Baron de Staël had reopened the Swedish embassy, and she saw no obstacle to her giving an impressive performance with Benjamin as her leading man.

Contemplating the departure of his daughter, Necker confessed he had a few misgivings. "Don't forget all the trouble you got into once before," he warned her. "Don't be too ambitious until you're living in a country where you can say and write what you please. And let me hope that Monsieur Constant won't urge you to take any extreme position; he would do well to give you a lesson or two in prudence and caution."

Like Necker, Mathieu de Montmorency feared the worst. Learning of a riot in Paris on the 20th of May, he trembled for Germaine's safety. Had she turned back in time? "I can only write you of my misgivings and of my most painful suspicions," he informed her cousin Madame Necker de Saussure. "My imagination runs wild when I think of the town in which Madame de Staël *may* have heard of this latest and most frightful uprising. I wonder whether she stopped short in the provinces or was she so rash as to go on her way. She did promise us that she'd turn back at the first news of anything wrong."

Germaine continued on her way. She was frank to admit she had been meeting with aristocrats who had been banished from France. When she was denounced in the Paris press for her activities, she bravely answered her accusers. "I sincerely wish for the establishment of the French Republic on the sacred foundation of justice and humanity," she declared.

She would be heard. In 1794 she had published a pamphlet, *Reflections on Peace, Intended for Mr. Pitt and the French People*, in which she pointed out that it was to the immediate interest of France as well as England to put an end to the revolutionary wars. Now she reasoned that the times called for the re-establishment of absolute monarchy. Such a government, she calculated, would have the enthusiastic support of a great number of people, whereas in the past it would have had no backing whatsoever. She dreaded the thought of government in the hands of men of no property; such a situation could only lead to the horrors of Robespierre. Men of no property might have something to offer the country, but they were better off when playing no political role. She was positive that the right to hold private property was essential to any moderate regime.

In her convictions concerning private property she was not alone. The committee that was inventing the next French constitution had come to the conclusion that universal suffrage should be abolished. Furthermore, the members of the legislature, the committee decided, should be over thirty years old and should be required to meet a property qualification.

When the Directory, as the new government was called, was launched on the 27th of October, 1795, Germaine did not need to be told that Paul-François-Nicholas Comte de Barras was the shrewdest of the five directors sharing the executive responsibility. This dissolute Provençal had the sense to send for Napoleon Bonaparte when the advent of the Directory was threatened by a royalist insurrection. The young general had been instrumental in the capture of the port of Toulon by the revolutionary troops in 1793. In dealing with the royalist rioters in Paris he was ruthless. Gathering his forces at the Church of Saint-Roch in the rue Saint-Honoré, Napoleon annihilated the counterrevolutionaries on the 4th of October, or the 13th Vendémiaire.

It was evident that peace, of a kind, was returning to France. Germaine saw no reason why Benjamin should delay making a commitment. "To put your paternal concern at rest," she notified Juste Constant six days after Napoleon settled matters on the rue Saint-Honoré, "let me tell you that Benjamin has just made a very good investment in the national securities, and that he stands to receive an income of ten thousand pounds or so a year."

This was considerate of Germaine, but the very thought of any collaboration between her and Benjamin was distasteful to Mathieu de Montmorency. "What a terrible influence Paris will have over her," he wrote Madame Necker de Saussure. "Benjamin too will have a dreadful influence over her. I have an obligation, and I must face it: I must see to it that she is not swept into the current."

Sick at heart, Mathieu set out for Paris, which was not the wisest decision of his life. He was arrested as a notorious royalist, even though Germaine went to the trouble of hiding him in the Swedish embassy, and he was only released after Marie-Joseph-Blaise de Chénier, the dramatist, intervened on his behalf. As for Germaine herself, she was not received so warmly as she would have preferred. Threatened with banishment by the Committee of Public Safety, she was tolerated only after the Baron de Staël appealed to the government, and at last, in December, 1795, she retreated to Switzerland to plan the next invasion.

Germaine could not be idle. She devoted her leisure to the writing of a pamphlet on the influence of passion on the happiness of individuals and nations. This was not one of her important works, but she was pleased to prove that she was still a disciple of Jean-Jacques Rousseau. The thought of a happy marriage moved her to ecstasy, and she also pointed out that children and wise men are much alike. "The greatest achievement of reason," she declared, "is to recall us to a state of nature."

In the meantime Benjamin contrived to publish a leaflet on the strength of the new government. This was termed "unwanted rubbish" by a journalist in Paris. Benjamin at once challenged him to a duel. The affair ended in a reconciliation, but the disgruntled author came to understand he must establish French citizenship if he were to play a political role in Paris. He began by establishing a French domicile. Running back to Necker at Coppet for the funds, he purchased the ruined abbey of Hérivaux near the Parisian suburb of Luzarches. He also persuaded Barras that Germaine might once more be allowed in France, and by the end of 1796 the two of them were comfortably installed in the ruined abbey.

Once again Mathieu was distressed. "You have torn away the veil from before my eyes," he wrote Madame Necker de Saussure, "by making plain that there is a danger inherent in Constant's return to France which you have judged more accurately than I. If she surrenders, if she makes her preference for him more explicit and notorious every day, there is nothing I can dream of that would make me more unhappy. I am overcome with grief."

Mathieu guessed, but Mathieu did not know. In the spring of 1797 Germaine was mortified to learn that her husband, who had once more been recalled as ambassador, might not be able to provide her with a roof. "I've been told," she wrote him, "that you are giving more and more consideration to renting your house. Perhaps you have forgotten that I am pregnant, and that I can't give birth on the street. In the name of my father and of your children, I beg you to behave. . . . I've had all kinds of trouble getting here, I'm pregnant, I'm exiled from Paris, I'm chained to this place, and you're in Paris and don't ever come to see me; you're even ready, I believe, to sell my bed without saying a word to me."

At this very moment Benjamin was beginning to realize that Germaine was a demanding woman. "I'm writing," he said in a letter to his aunt Madame de Nassau, "to ask if you can't help me out of the difficulty I am in. A connection which I look upon as a duty, or if you will, as a weakness, but a connection that I'll keep up until a real obligation frees me from it, and that I can only put an end to by admitting that I'm terribly weary of it, but too polite to say so—this connection, which can only be severed by a jolt that I couldn't think of giving the person I'm describing, has had me in chains now for two years."

A little later Benjamin was taking a new look at his situation. Germaine, he said, had given him "a new and remarkable proof of her devotion." On the 8th of June, 1797, she gave birth to Edwige-Gustavine-Albertine, or Albertine, as the child was usually known.

Germaine's motherhood could not keep her from advancing the cause of Benjamin. She took him to call on Barras. "Here's an enormously clever man," she reminded the Director, "and he's a person who belongs on our side. He's absolutely devoted to our cause."

The memoirs of Barras indicate that he found Benjamin stupid, affected, and effeminate, and Germaine unbearably mannish. But Benjamin, no matter how chilling the atmosphere, did as he was told. "Citoyen Directeur," he began, "I should be happy indeed if the tract which I take the liberty of offering you should find favor in your eyes."

"He is a good citizen," Germaine went on, "a man who has the courage to think straight. Just take a look at the title of his pamphlet, *Of the Strength of the Present Government in France, and of the Necessity for Joining It.*

"This pamphlet will bring you any number of adherents; it will be worth several battalions to you; Citoyen Directeur, it's time to take what I'm saying seriously, and not stand on ceremony. There is no question at all that an author who lets a government know how strong it is, and reveals this strength to those who deny it exists, such an author deserves something better than having his eyes scratched out."

Benjamin was one man she pressed on Barras. Another was Talleyrand, who had, she knew, been languishing in the United States since their last meeting at Juniper Hall. The Bishop was not enchanted by the society of Philadelphia. "There's a lot of money to be made here," he wrote Germaine in the spring of 1794, "but mostly by those who already have money on hand." Shortly after this he complained that "if I spend another year here, I'll be in my grave." A year later he announced that his mind was definitely made up. "There will either be an earthquake from one end of Europe to the other, or I'll be back next May."

Germaine did more than encourage Talleyrand in his desire to return to the Old World. In the fall of 1795 she was so wise as to cultivate Eugénie de la Bouchardie, a woman who sang to the accompaniment of her harp and who happened to be a close friend of Marie-Joseph-Blaise de Chénier. She saw to it that the harpist sang "The Ballad of the Exile" in Chénier's presence. The dramatist was touched. On the 4th of September he took care that Talleyrand's name was removed from the list of those who had been banished from France.

"You've done absolutely everything I asked for," the Bishop wrote Germaine from America. "I love you with all my heart." On the 13th of June, 1796, he set sail from Philadelphia. He tarried in Hamburg, but not for long. Early in the summer of 1797 he was a prominent member of a constitutional club, or Cercle Constitutionnel, that Benjamin had helped to launch.

Of Talleyrand's meeting with Barras there are two accounts. According to his own version Talleyrand called on the Director on the very day one of Barras' closest friends was found drowned. The Bishop expressed his sympathy; the Director was so deeply moved that he broke into tears. "The embarrassment which he experienced in the presence of a man like myself, whom he did not know at all, gradually vanished, and the concern that I revealed seemed to do him some good," wrote Talleyrand in his memoirs. Barras "was a man of passion, all energy. In the less than two hours that passed since we met, I was beginning to read his mind."

Very likely the Bishop was not exaggerating when he claimed he saw through the Director. He was also more benevolent than his opponent. "That insignificant, expressionless, chalklike face of his, and the relentless stare of his inanimate eyes made me believe that Robespierre had come back to life," wrote Barras of his first glimpse of Talleyrand. He claimed he said as much to Germaine, who had come to introduce her old friend in person.

"Oh," said Germaine—again according to Barras's version—"I can tell you that the resemblance is not perfect." Then she turned to the Bishop. "Why, Citoyen Talleyrand, we were just talking about you. I had no idea of flattering you when I claimed you were a faithful friend."

Whereupon, if we are to believe Barras once more, Talleyrand became the very personification of humility. "Your respectful servant, your grateful servant," he murmured, "I'm none the less respectful for being grateful, and only my admiration can hope to match my respect and my gratitude."

"I've really told you nothing yet about Citoyen Talleyrand," Germaine seems to have said as she brought the interview to a close. "I might embarrass that modest man, and I can only talk to you about him when he isn't around; I'll come back tomorrow by myself. I must have a private audience with you."

Barras's recollection of his next meeting with Germaine is quotable, even if possibly unreliable.

Talleyrand "has all the vices of the *ancien régime* and of the *nouveau régime*," she is supposed to have made plain. "He has always had and he always will have an entry into every political party. For that very reason you can't possibly find a more useful agent. As for you, Citoyen Directeur, he is so fond of you, he respects you so deeply, that he looks upon you as superhuman. It is you, and you alone, whom he is anxious to serve. I'm telling you everything that's on his mind, because I feel exactly the same way." According to Barras, she pointed out that Talleyrand would have to be in his good graces, because he would be at odds with all his other colleagues. "As he'll be completely dependent upon your favors, he'll have to take his orders from you."

The Director was beginning to understand that the Bishop was a candidate for one of the highest offices in the power of the government. Barras has written that Germaine paid yet another frantic visit. "Can you guess what's going on?" she is said to have cried out. "I've just left him this minute; perhaps he is no longer among the living. He let me know he'd throw himself into the Seine if you didn't make him Minister of Foreign Affairs."

This was exactly what Barras was about to do. On the 18th of July, 1797, with the backing of Barras and two other Directors, Charles-Maurice de Talleyrand-Périgord entered upon the career for which he was so exquisitely suited.

Germaine was not so vulgar as to believe that she had made history. But she could be forgiven if she imagined that her opinions would be respected in high places.

CHAPTER SEVEN

THE
UNCONQUERABLE
HORIZON

On the day that Talleyrand took command of the foreign policy of France, Germaine had not yet met the most important man in the world. She had, however, read with rapture the news of Napoleon's conquest of Italy, and she knew that her life would not be complete until she stood face to face with the man who was hurrying the death of the century that had failed to appreciate her father.

She wrote to Napoleon during the Italian campaign. The text of her letters has not been preserved, but the contents may be imagined from the recollections of Napoleon's followers. She is supposed to have compared the conqueror to both Scipio and Tancred, and to have expressed her regret that such a genius was mated to "an insignificant little Creole" who could not hope to understand him. According to Louis-Antoine-Fauvelet de Bourrienne, who was with the general at the time, Napoleon was unwilling to believe that providence intended he should be worshipped by a "soul on fire," as Germaine described herself.

"Can you make anything of all this nonsense?" Napoleon asked Bourrienne. "That woman is insane . . . that bluestocking has dared to compare herself to Josephine. . . . I won't answer her letters."

Although no answer came from the other side of the Alps, Germaine was not discouraged. She lent her approval to the 18th Fructidor, as the coup d'état of the 4th of September, 1797, was known. Harried by royalists and moderates, the desperate Directors begged Napoleon for assistance. He dispatched Pierre Augureau (later known as the Duc de Castiglione), who canceled the elections in forty-nine departments and arranged for a number of stubborn men to be deported to French Guiana. Whether Germaine was altogether pleased by the outcome is a question. Her friends insisted that she hadn't wished for the 19th Fructidor, but only the 18th.

In the meantime Germaine hoped against hope that Napoleon would become aware of the world that her imagination was ready to construct. She decided that his prose was noble, and she detected a pleasing moderation in his conduct. Moreover, she was overjoyed to learn that he, like herself, was an admirer of the epic poetry of Ossian.

At last, on the 5th of December, 1797, came the occasion that Germaine had longed for. Napoleon arrived in Paris with the Treaty of Campo Formio under his arm. Belgium and the left bank of the Rhine were now French territory. This was a fact of which Talleyrand was happy to take notice. He agreed to receive the general the next morning at eleven, and he invited Germaine to witness the reception. At ten she was on hand.

For once she was distraught. "I didn't know exactly what to say," she wrote, "when he came over to tell me that he had tried to see my father at Coppet, and was sorry he had gone through Switzerland without having called on him. But when I had slightly recovered from my embarrassment and my admiration, I grew quite afraid of him.

"At this time Bonaparte had no real authority; there were even those who supposed he had fallen out of favor with the Directory. The fear he inspired wherever he went could be attributed only to the power of his personality. I had known men with the highest ideals, and men with the lowest, but the impression that Bonaparte made on me could not be compared with that produced by either extreme. He was not calm, he was not excitable, he was not generous, he was not mean—at least like anyone I had ever seen. Such a man, who had not his equal, could neither love nor be loved. He was more than a man—or less. Not only his bearing, but his manner of thinking and his choice of words proved that he was a foreigner—which made it all the easier for him to intimidate the French.

"Far from being reassured, the more I saw of Bonaparte, the more disturbed I became. In a vague way I sensed that he was a man who had no emotions. To him a human being was a fact or a thing, not someone to be treated as an equal. He was a clever chess player set to checkmate the human race. His triumphs were due as much to his defects as to his real abilities. Compassion could never throw him off his course; neither could the charms of any individual, the claims of any religion, nor the belief in any idea. . . .

"Every time I listened to him, I was struck by the power of his intelligence—which could not be compared for a second with the kind of mind we expect from educated and cultivated men in France and England. But when he began to speak, he showed he could seize an opportunity as effortlessly as a hunter bagging his game. Now and then he could really be entertaining when talking about the political and military crises he had survived; he even exhibited a streak of Italian imagination when telling amusing stories. But nothing could overcome my distaste for the man. . . . He despised the people, on whose support he counted, and he did not know the meaning of the word enthusiasm, even though he set out to astonish mankind."

Germaine was there on the 10th of December, when the Directory held an official reception for Napoleon in the courtyard of the Luxembourg palace. An altar of the nation had been erected, smothered with trophies and flags captured by the Army of Italy, and the Directors donned something resembling Roman togas for the occasion. The dramatist Chénier recited a hymn he had written in the conqueror's honor, and Talleyrand was moved to mention "the insatiable passion for humanity" displayed by the French troops.

Germaine watched; Germaine listened. She also listened when she came across Napoleon in society. She ventured to ask him who, in his opinion, was the first woman of the world. "The woman who has had the most children," came the answer. When she inquired if he liked women, he replied: "Madame, I love my wife." For a second she admitted that Napoleon was sublime. "Epaminondas might have given an answer like that," she reflected.

But her unfavorable impression of Napoleon was reinforced when she had dinner with him and the Abbé Sieyès, a renegade from the Church who was working his way into the heart of the Directory. Recalling this meeting, Germaine wrote that "whenever Napoleon discovered that anyone was staring at him, he immediately extinguished the last sign of life in his eyes, which turned to marble. At such a moment there would be no expression at all on his face, except for a vague smile that would now and then play over his lips, baffling anyone who hoped to read his mind. . . .

"Sieyès kept coming right to the point, which was just what you would expect from a man of his intelligence. He left no doubt of the esteem in which he held my father. Necker, he said, was the only man who had ever brought the imagination of a poet to bear on the exact calculations of a great financier. I was pleased to hear him praise my father; he knew what he was talking about. General Bonaparte, who heard all this, also had a few kind words to say about my father and me, but he talked like someone who is only interested in getting what he can out of people."

Germaine was saddened by the discovery that Napoleon did not understand the greatness of Necker. A little later she found herself in a serious argument with the conqueror on the subject of the suffrage in her own Swiss canton. Making the most of his reputation as the defender of the French Revolution, he dared to suggest that it was unfair to exclude any portion of the inhabitants from the government. "All that is very well as a matter of principle," Germaine conceded, "but it is also true that men must win their freedom by their own efforts, and not by calling in a foreign power which must have the upper hand." With this he flatly disagreed; the forces the Directory sent to occupy Switzerland were not removed.

Having lost this argument, Germaine could be forgiven for emphasizing in her recollections another woman's stand against Napoleon. "Madame," the general informed the lady in question, "I don't want women mixed up in politics." "You are perfectly right," came the reply, "but in a country where their heads are cut off, it is only natural for them to want to know why."

Returning to Coppet in the summer of 1798, Germaine must have been disappointed to discover that her father did not share all her misgivings. Necker had learned that Napoleon was reading *On the Influence of*

Passion at the height of the Egyptian campaign. "Your reputation is now assured on the banks of the Nile," he told his daughter. "Alexander the Great sent for sophists and philosophers from all over the world, so that he could enjoy their conversation. The Corsican Alexander, to save time, gets in touch with only one mind, that of Madame de Staël. *He knows what's going on.*"

For a banker, Necker was optimistic. Napoleon may have read this essay, he may even have enjoyed it, but he needed the advice of no one when it came to rhetoric. "Soldiers, from these pyramids forty centuries of history look down upon you!" was a command issued on his own responsibility. And he made his own plans when the Egyptian campaign did not turn out as he intended. On the 8th of October, 1799, he was back in France. On the 9th of November (or 18th Brumaire) he and Sieyès overthrew the Directory, setting up the Consulate under which Napoleon was to be First Consul for the term of ten years. This coup d'état was ratified by a plebiscite that gave the general a majority of three million votes.

Napoleon had no need of Germaine on the 18th Brumaire. He had even less need of her on the 14th of June, 1800, when he won a major victory over the Austrian armies at Marengo. Germaine confessed that Marengo was an achievement that could turn anyone's head. "I myself gave way to enthusiasm," she wrote. "The friends of the government will be satisfied with my conduct this winter—that is, if they can be satisfied with admiration instead of flattery." At Coppet Necker prayed for restraint. "Now your hero Bonaparte is a god in everyone's eyes," he noted, recalling her adulation in other days. "Prudence is called for."

More than prudence was required. At the very beginning of the year Napoleon had insisted on the publication of a piece of advice in the *Moniteur* or *Gazette*

Nationale. "We all yearn for fame, but some people don't understand that a wise man doesn't make his way by gushing, but by serving, even in an obscure position, the public which in the last analysis renders the real decisions." On the same day *Le Peuple* reminded Germaine that "it's not your fault if you're ugly, but you are responsible if you mix in politics. It is time you learned your lesson; your kingdom is no longer of this world. You know the way to Switzerland. If you don't want to get in trouble, get on the road."

But Germaine could not leave, could not give up all hope of making a lasting impression on the First Consul. "You know," she told his brother Lucien, "I really am stupid in his presence. It's because I want so much to please him. I have no idea of what I'm saying, I try one attack and then another, I want so much to force him to pay attention to me. Well, the result is that I become as silly as a goose."

Eagerly she cultivated Napoleon's other brother Joseph. "I wonder why a man of good taste like yourself doesn't take the trouble to answer a woman's letters?" she asked. "Why a man who is really so kind is so curt when it comes to appreciating the most heartfelt gratitude he has ever inspired?"

A little later she was singing a hymn of praise to Joseph's country seat at Mortfontaine. "Although," she wrote, "you have teased me about my liking for city life, I must tell you that I miss Mortfontaine day and night, and when I saw the sun come up today, I kept thinking that I might be walking with you in your beautiful garden, for you must know that your being there is the most charming thing of all."

She was not easily discouraged. "Won't you sign a treaty of peace with me?" she asked Joseph. "Won't you come to see me this morning or this evening? I'll be alone. Won't you come to lunch tomorrow and bring your friends?" When the time drew near for the peace of Amiens, she could no longer restrain herself. "Peace with England will bring happiness to the entire world. You are in charge of the most important negotiations in the history of France."

Joseph might smile, but Napoleon remained stern. "Monsieur de Staël," he wrote Joseph, "is in the greatest distress, and his wife goes around giving dinners and balls. If you go on seeing her, wouldn't it be a good idea if you got that woman to give her husband an allowance of 1,000 or 2,000 francs a month? Where on earth would we be in these times if decent people had no morals at all and scoffed at the sacred ties that bind children to their fathers and mothers? The moral standards of Madame de Staël must be judged just as if she were a man—a man about to inherit the fortune of Monsieur Necker, a man who had enjoyed all his life the privileges attached to a great name, and a man who let his wife live in poverty while he kept up the highest style. Do you think you would care to be intimate with such a man?"

"If you'd only show her a little kindness, she'd fall down at your feet," Joseph once informed his brother. "I've had enough of that!" said Napoleon. "I don't want to have anything to do with that kind of hero worship. Besides, she's too ugly."

Germaine did her best when she met the First Consul at General Berthier's residence, but her best was not enough. Although she had thought up all kinds of things to say for the occasion, Napoleon barely noticed her. For her part she observed that he stood on one foot and then on the other after dinner, "just like the princes of the House of Bourbon. I pointed out to a neighbor that his royal traits were already manifest."

By then it was obvious that Napoleon could never become one of her admirers. "Warn that woman," he told Lucien and Joseph, "that I am no Louis XVI. . . . Tell her she must never stand in my way. If she does, I'll smash her. I'll break her. The only practical thing for her to do is to keep her mouth shut." Apparently he had been unusually irritated by the reports of a talk that Joseph had had with her not long after the 18th Brumaire. "My brother has been complaining about you," Joseph informed Germaine. "Why in the world, he repeated to me yesterday, does Madame de Staël want to stand aloof from the government? What does she want? The repayment of her father's loan to the treasury? I'll take care of that. Permission to stay in Paris? I'll take care of that. But what, exactly, does she want?" To this she made a fatal answer. "You know very well," she said, "that it's not a question of what I want, but of what thoughts I happen to have in my head."

Benjamin Constant would have been the first to applaud this declaration. Under the Consulate he became exceedingly anxious for an appointment to the Tribunate, an assembly presumably constituted to discuss legal questions, and he succeeded in winning this honor before the year 1799 was over. His interview with Napoleon had been most satisfactory. "You know," he declared, "that I am your man. I'm not one of those ideologues who deal in airy generalizations. I am a matter-of-fact man, and if you nominate me, you can count on me." A little later, in talking to Sieyès, he made plain that after all he had certain reservations on the subject of the First Consul. "You know," he pointed out, "how much I hate brute force. I can never be an admirer of a soldier. I insist on principles, I insist on ideals, and I insist on justice. And if I get your vote, you can count on me, for I am Napoleon's worst enemy."

This was a point which he set out to prove in no uncertain terms. Learning that the First Consul intended to impose a time limit on debates in the Tribunate, he decided that in his very first speech he would take his stand against this arbitrary ruling. The evening before his début he defined, for Germaine's benefit, the importance of the gesture. She was in the midst of one of her splendid dinners; the guests were persons whom no sane man could afford to neglect. "Your salon," he exclaimed, "is filled with people who interest you. If I give my speech, it will be empty tomorrow. Think it over." Germaine's answer was no surprise. "You must," she said, "be faithful to your convictions."

On the next morning, the 5th of January, 1800, Benjamin arose in the Tribunate and alluded to the impatience of the First Consul. The members of the assembly, he said, were being given the summary treatment of an enemy army. The reaction to his words was immediate, and it was exactly what he had anticipated. On that very afternoon five out of ten guests expected at Germaine's next party sent their regrets. What was equally remarkable, Joseph, on his brother's orders, stopped paying his calls.

Over a year went by before Benjamin was removed (with twenty other men with opinions of their own) from the Tribunate, but Napoleon lost no time in letting it be known that everyone who went into Madame de Staël's house came out less convinced of the justice of his cause.

This was a compliment, coming from the most important man in the world. Yet the report was troubling. Equally troubling—whether Germaine was ever aware of what was going on, we have no way of knowing— was the sudden attachment that Benjamin had formed with a certain Anne-Suzanne Lindsay. Born at Calais, the daughter of Jeremy O'Dwyer, an innkeeper who had served with a British regiment on the Continent, Anne-Suzanne had been adopted as a little girl by none other than the Duchesse de Fitz-James. Mysteriously discarded by this great patroness, she had been taken up by one man after another, including the future Count of Melfort and Perth, who left her for an heiress. Then she had shone in Hyde Park as the mistress of Auguste de Lamoignon, son of the Keeper of the Seals of France. She returned from England at the beginning of the Consulate, and in October, 1800, met Benjamin at the house of Julie Talma, the wife of the tragedian.

For four years Benjamin and Anne-Suzanne exchanged letters, and once, in one message, he cried out: "My dearest, you love me, give yourself completely to me, or I'll die." These are the facts, and if this were all, Anne-Suzanne would be no more than a footnote to Benjamin's biography, a relief from the ambitious embraces of Germaine. But this was not all. For when Benjamin came to write *Adolphe*, the novel that has fixed his reputation as a pitiless observer of his own love affairs, he turned to Anne-Suzanne—even more than to Charlotte, the Baroness of Marenholz—for the creation of his heroine Ellénore.

In its essence *Adolphe* is the record of Benjamin's failure to respond to the passion Anne-Suzanne lavished upon him. For this failure he reproached himself again and again; the novel ends with Ellénore's despair. "Is there any country where I wouldn't follow you?" she asks. "Can you conceive of any place I wouldn't hide in, just to be with you, without being a burden to you? But no, you'll have none of this. Every plan that I bring up, timid and trembling person that I am, you cast superbly aside. All that I can hope for is your silence."

Germaine was in need of consolation at this time. In 1798 she had fortunately met Juliette Récamier, the wife of an unusually opulent banker from Lyons. Juliette would follow her to the end.

The theory has been advanced, by Juliette's scholarly biographer Edouard Herriot, that she was the daughter as well as the wife of her husband. The marriage, so the theory runs, was arranged to protect her person and her fortune during the Revolution. If there be any truth in this—the anxiety of such a situation needs no emphasis—it may explain why this enchantress apparently never surrendered to anyone, even though her beauty and her charm were immediately apparent to the several distinguished men who became her abject servants, not for an afternoon but for life.

Juliette has told the story of her first meeting with Germaine; at the time her husband was about to purchase a house that Madame de Staël owned on the Chaussée d'Antin. "Monsieur Récamier," she said, "came in with a lady whose name I was not given, and with whom he left me alone while he went out to join some friends in the garden. She was oddly dressed, very casually, and was wearing a tiny hat decked out with flowers. I took her for a foreigner. When she glanced at me, I was struck by the beauty of her eyes. I couldn't exactly understand what came over me, but there is no doubt that I was trying harder to recognize her and to place her than I was in making her feel at home. Then she told me, and I shall never forget this moment, that she was really delighted to make my acquaintance, and that Monsieur Necker, her father . . . With that I knew she was Madame de Staël. I didn't listen to the rest of the sentence. I blushed, and I lost all my composure.

"I had just finished reading her *Letters on Rousseau*, and I was in love with the book. I couldn't express my feelings in words; I could only look at her. I was frightened, and yet I fell immediately under her spell. Anyone could see that she was completely at ease, the kind of woman one meets only once in a lifetime. She was staring at me with her big eyes, but I could see that she was just as kind as she was considerate. She paid me a number of compliments on my figure, which might have been too much of a good thing, but weren't, for I could tell that her remarks were completely unrehearsed. All this made her praise all the more sweet to my ears. . . . I was terribly embarrassed, but she didn't seem to mind; she understood the state I was in. She told me she wanted to see me the next time she was in Paris. She was then about to leave for Coppet.

"She left an unforgettable impression on me. From that day forward I could think of nothing but Madame de Staël, so completely had I fallen under the influence of her strong and passionate nature."

Germaine was to come again and again to visit Juliette in the Chaussée d'Antin. Passing through the great courtyard, she entered what appears to have been one of the noble interiors of Napoleonic Paris. It was on the bedroom that the architect Berthault devoted his most scrupulous attention when he remodeled the house, and it was her bedroom that Juliette made a point of displaying to all her sure friends. The boiserie was exquisite; the mirrors have been immortalized in the memoirs of Johann Friedrich Reichardt, a German who was a frequent guest. The walls were one costly mirror after another, and Juliette could lie in her antique bed (the bed of a goddess, thought Reichardt) and be reflected from tip to toe. As if the mirrors were not sufficiently splendid, two giant candelabra, each with half a dozen branches, lit up the white curtains of the bedstead and the violet damask hangings at the other end of the room. Nor was this all. Juliette's bathroom was an equally eloquent advertisement of the Récamier fortune, a superb parade of mirrors and satin. The tub itself could be quickly transformed into a sofa covered with red Morocco leather.

Germaine may have sought out, day after day, the splendors of the Récamier mansion, but she did so only after satisfying her Genevan conscience. In 1800 she published the first of her important works, *Literature Considered in Its Relation to Social Institutions*. The conclusion left no doubt that she was her father's daughter. "What a blessing from heaven morality is!" she wrote. "Morality helps us to understand all that is good in nature, and morality alone gives permanence and repose to all that we enjoy on earth. What we admire in great men is after all the fact that their high ideals have been recognized."

But *Literature* was more than a tract. It was also more than a plea for the emancipation of women, even though Germaine pointed out "as soon as a woman is known to be exceptional, the public turns against her. The common people judge everything by what is tried and true, and would never dream of having an opinion of their own. . . . It's only too obvious that a man has no obligation whatever to a woman who is considered brilliant. To such a woman a man can be ungrateful, treacherous, and even mean, and no one will think of taking her side."

Literature was also more than a polemic directed against Napoleon, although Germaine could not refrain from reminding the French people that "once military men dominated a nation, scorning philosophy and belles-lettres, there was no hope of enlightenment."

In its essence *Literature* was a manifesto of the coming romantic movement in France. Germaine may have been absurd at times in her survey reaching from the age of Pericles to the nineteenth century, but the launchers of manifestoes have always exaggerated their claims, well aware that to be intemperate is to be noticed. She was glib, but cannily so, when she announced that "the Greeks, no matter how remarkable they may have been, are not really missed." Or when she dared to say that "the innumerable faults one can find in Dante must be blamed on the century he lived in." Or when she agreed that "sandy stretches and incoherent images" are easily discovered in Shakespeare's plays.

As a child of the unpoetic eighteenth century Germaine could not help thinking that "poetry of all the arts is the most reasonable." But as a prophet of the nineteenth she went on to explain that "again and again in this work I have emphasized everything which can prove the perfectibility of the human race. This is no empty theory. A close observation of the facts has led me to this conclusion."

Not every romantic shared this conviction. François-René Vicomte de Chateaubriand, who had so far published merely an historical, political, and moral essay on the subject of revolution, presumed to question Germaine on the subject of the infinite improvement of the human race. Writing to his friend Fontanes (the letter was printed in the *Mercure*) he declared that "Madame de Staël endows philosophy with powers that I attribute only to religion. You know of course that my obsession is to see Jesus Christ everywhere, while Madame de Staël talks of nothing but perfectibility. . . . I am sorry that she has not given a religious interpretation of the power of our emotions. In my opinion perfectibility is of no help at all when we come to judge human weaknesses. . . .

"Sometimes Madame de Staël seems to be a Christian; a second later she is the victim of philosophy. Now and then, inspired by her natural sensitivity, she speaks with the noble accent which is all her own, but suddenly she gets involved in arguments and no longer listens to the beating of her heart. . . .

"The book is a curious mixture of truth and error. . . . Here is what I should dare to tell her, if I had the honor of her acquaintance. There is no doubt that you are an unusual woman. You have a good mind, and your powers of imagination are often charming indeed. . . . Often you express yourself nobly and forcefully. But in spite of all these delightful attributes, this work of yours is far from the book it might have been. Your style is monotonous, and you use far too many metaphysical terms. Many of your readers will be annoyed by the conscious subtlety of your reasoning, others will be disappointed by your scholarship, or lack of it, and what you take to be a philosophy is only a narrow point of view. That is how I should address Madame de Staël if I were thinking of her reputation in the years to come. I might go on to say: you do not seem to be a happy woman; again and again you complain that you are misunderstood. The truth is that there are certain people who never cease searching in vain for those who will understand them. Do you imagine that philosophy can ever relieve you of the tedium of existence? A desert is likely to remain a desert until the end of time."

If this letter had come from a mere critic, it might have been ignored, but no one could overlook Chateaubriand, and Germaine realized that his comments were those of a poet who could become a friend. They met, to become friends forever. Nor was there a second of tension, possibly because passion played no part in their encounters.

Chateaubriand may have been the most distinguished man that Germaine ever met; he is certainly the most difficult to introduce to an Anglo-Saxon audience. He was, and this may be said without indulging in hyperbole, the greatest rhetorician in the history of French literature. This is a dangerous tribute to pay in England or America where rhetoric is a dubious commodity, nor will the cause of Chateaubriand be advanced by admitting that he was a most impractical man. When he set

sail for America in 1791 he was in search of the North-
west Passage; anyone could point out that the futility
of such a quest had already been exposed by La Pérouse
and Cook. Such a traveler could never be a shrewd
statesman. He has been criticized for provoking the
French invasion of Spain in the days of the Restoration,
and other men may have been better ambassadors for
France in Berlin and London. Finally, he may even be
considered absurd for lavishing on the foolish leaders of
the House of Bourbon a loyalty that they never deserved.

Chateaubriand himself might have agreed that the
Bourbons were not worth his devotion. But he had, he
felt, struck a perfect attitude, and he knew that the
poetry of his loyalty to a lost cause would win him admirers no matter what the trend of French politics in
the years to come. He may also have been aware of the
fact that his apology for the Roman Catholic Church,
making so much of the aesthetic aspect of the rites,
would be deplored by earnest theologians. What did it
matter if once again he had struck an ideal attitude?

But his greatest gift was his discovery of the truth
that man is what man remembers. He chose to remember only the superb moments of his life, and his memoirs
will never be matched.

Although Stendhal was angered by the rich prose
of the *Mémoires d'Outre-Tombe*, and although André
Gide succeeded in freeing himself from Chateaubriand's
spell, from generation to generation the master has enchanted authors who have won a certain reputation.
Gérard de Nerval owes much to him, and so does Baudelaire. As for Maurice Barrès, he patently modeled
the style of his greater tales and novels on that of Germaine's friend. But the most eloquent disciple of all is
Marcel Proust. The last pages of *Du Côté de Chez
Swann*, in which he insists that our recollection of a

certain image is merely our longing for a certain second, could only have been written by someone who recalled Chateaubriand's promenades in Rome.

Germaine seems to have sensed that her new acquaintance would reach an exceptional audience. She presumed to console him on the death of the Comtesse de Beaumont, a woman to whom he had given more than affection. "My dear Francis," she wrote, "give me a place in your life. I admire you, I loved the woman for whom you are mourning. I am a devoted friend. I shall be a sister to you." It was only natural, since her interest in his career was so keen, that she should worry over the chapter devoted to virginity in his *Génie du Christianisme*. "Oh, dear," she told her circle. "Our poor Chateaubriand! This will fall flat."

Germaine need not have worried. The publication of *Le Génie de Christianisme* proved that the Roman Catholic Church had no more persuasive defender in Napoleonic France. Moreover, one of the chapters from this work, the tale of *Attala*, had already met an instant success.

Chauteaubriand was enjoying his first fame when he called on Germaine one morning to find Juliette Récamier at her side. Juliette was an apparition on which he had not counted. "I had never conceived of anything comparable," he noted in his memoirs.

CHAPTER EIGHT

DELPHINE

———————◆———————

T H E R E came a time when Germaine could not resist asking Talleyrand if Napoleon were intelligent.
"You know, of course," she said, "that I have some idea
of what intelligence is all about. Tell me, in your opinion, is he as intelligent as I am?" "He isn't as brave as
you are," Talleyrand replied.

An interesting advertisement of Germaine's bravery
was the publication in December, 1802, of her first
novel *Delphine*. In the preface she made plain that the
intellectual climate of Napoleonic France left much to
be desired, and that as long as the First Consul remained
in power literary criticism could not amount to much
more than calculated insults or the puffs of hacks. She
decided that "writers who have any idea of expressing
what is on their minds must discount in advance anything that happens to be said about their work. They
must," she went on, "address the future not the present,
for they are writing for a France which is enlightened,
but silent."

This declaration of independence must have been a

surprise to Necker. He had recently written the First Consul that his daughter "may have been slow to comprehend that a certain prudence is advisable under the new state of affairs. But I should prefer to let bygones be bygones and ask the Consul to overlook anything that may not have pleased him. I am positive that from this day forward Madame de Staël will behave with the most perfect circumspection. My daughter has just given me her word that she will lead the kind of life that you will tell her to lead, and that she will no longer indulge in any conversation touching on government or politics. She can easily select other subjects for the play of her wit."

Necker could persuade himself that his daughter was a new woman, but no one else could imagine that Germaine had reformed. Paris expected that *Delphine* would be an indiscreet novel, and Paris was not disappointed. As one journalist wrote in the *Journal de Paris:* "Do you know why there wasn't a soul to be seen in the theaters either the day before yesterday or yesterday, why there will be very few people at mass today (even though it's Sunday), why hack drivers complain they have had no business for the last two days, why almost every carriage in town is resting in the stables, and why, when all is said and done, there has been so much less going on in Paris since Sunday a week ago? The reason is that the whole town is staying home to read Madame de Staël's new novel. The preface alone called for three days of study and reflection. The rest of the book is even more engrossing. In a couple of days from now, everyone will be talking, reading, and writing about nothing but the pros and cons of Madame de Staël's book."

Everyone knew that Germaine loved not wisely but too well; everyone anticipated that she would reveal much and hint at more about her friends; everyone (with certain significant exceptions) was positive that she had written a *roman à clef* worth deciphering.

It was true that the Baron de Staël did not parade in the pages of *Delphine*, but then he had died only recently, in May, and Germaine had been saddened by his end. "In all my life I've never been so unhappy," she wrote a former attaché of the Swedish embassy. There may even have been a moment when she realized that she had not always been true to her husband. "In my novel," she pointed out in the preface, "I could not forgive Delphine for having given way to her feelings for a married man."

Germaine had indeed created an unhappy heroine, the victim, everyone agreed, of her perfidious friend Sophie de Vernon.

Madame de Vernon was a woman who wasted no time worrying over moral questions; she was interested in results alone. "Although she was endowed with the most splendid talents, success was the only thing that counted in her eyes, and whether an action was right or wrong was of no consequence at all to her."

"My convictions?" Madame de Vernon smiled when her young friend Delphine d'Albémar, a widow like herself, asked what she believed in. "No one knows what my convictions are, and as they have no influence whatever on my feelings, there is no reason, dear Delphine, for you to know what's in the back of my mind."

Delphine, who talked of nothing but morality, and with an enthusiasm that delighted all of her acquaintances, was pained to admit that Sophie de Vernon had two faults, a passion for gambling and a weakness for spending too much money. Yet Sophie's conversation was charming. "She didn't contradict a single idea of mine," Delphine recalled. "But she knew how to sway my opinion without my knowing what was going on."

Talleyrand, who was one of the devoted readers of

Delphine, savored above all the portrait of Madame de Vernon. "I am told," he said, "that Madame de Staël has put both of us in her novel. We are both disguised as women."

It was obvious that Delphine would have led a happier life if she had been a Protestant. Her Protestant admirer Henri de Lebensei, who was almost as clever as Benjamin Constant, pointed out that Calvinists enjoyed certain advantages. "I was born a Protestant," Lebensei reminded a friend. "I was not raised, I'll admit it, to respect the senseless and barbarous customs which force so many innocent people to sacrifice their natural affections. A proud man, a virtuous man, owes obedience to the spirit of universal morality, and to that alone."

Lebensei reminded this friend that "liberty is the only justification for the social order. History is dignified by triumphs of free peoples, and by them alone. The only names that ring through the centuries are the names of those who have loved liberty." There were those who feared that Lebensei might have been corrupted by the English—he had studied in Cambridge—but Delphine had no misgivings on that score. Neither did Lebensei's wife, who declared that "the English character is the noblest in the world."

Benjamin could not complain of the portrait Germaine had drawn of Henri de Lebensei, but neither could he forget that to know Germaine was to pay a price. "She has a real need for the language of love," he wrote in his diary, "a language I find it more and more difficult to speak with each day that passes. We'll be bound to quarrel; we'll be bound to go on our own ways. The longer our liaison lasts, the older we'll be; we'll be isolated, discontented, and we'll have forgotten how to take our pleasures elsewhere."

There were compensations; there were also tribulations. "No one," wrote Benjamin, "will ever appreciate my mind as completely as she does. No one will ever set me farther apart from the rest of humanity. But how busy she is! How absorbed she is! She has a man's mind and wants to be loved like a woman." He went on to admit that "Germaine has the makings in her for ten or twelve exceptional men . . . but she sets all her friends' teeth on edge. . . . She's the best creature on earth, but she's so restless and so subject to fits of melancholy that I can never lead a happy life in her shadow."

To his cousin Rosalie, Benjamin went into even greater detail. "I can understand, dear Rosalie," he told her, "your reluctance to discuss a person who is of some interest to both of us, and whose good and bad points sometimes provide the charm and again the horror of my existence. Now I should like you to conquer this reluctance. I beg you to do this out of your friendship for me; it's possibly the greatest and most important favor I could ask of you, and you are the only one who could do me such a favor at the most critical period of my life. You can count on it, that any letter you write will be burned two minutes after I've read it. Your name will never be mentioned. After all, I'm not eager for any explanation or any justification face to face. I'm the one who needs to hear from you, because I'm distressed by the grief I'm supposed to have caused her, and if I could find out that this grief doesn't exist, or that another object of interest could take its place at the very moment when people paint me pictures of her grief in the most horrid colors, then I could recover my sanity, and there would be an end to the remorse I feel, and I could become a free man again, sure that nothing could wreck all my plans and my life itself, not even the supernatural influence of her voice and her letters, nor the assurance that she can't live without me, and that I am responsible for her suffering."

A little later he wrote Rosalie that "with all her faults she's an excellent creature, and the most devoted and sensitive person in the world, even if her conduct often casts some doubt on her abilities. She's more easily upset than anyone I know, and the idea that I may have contributed to her grief is horribly painful to me. Nevertheless every day I feel more and more of a need for rest, for domestic life, and for having someone at my side whose happiness depends on me."

He had been writing to Germaine, but with many misgivings. "I don't tell her anything that isn't the truth, but I don't tell her the whole truth. The result is that she complains that my letters betray my indifference, and she'd accuse me of treachery if she saw my letter to you. The same thing would happen that's happened a hundred times before, and which, I believe, will always happen: I'd be condemned for the kind deed I'd committed, and for the grief I didn't want to bring upon her."

Benjamin could analyze his predicament. He could also understand that Germaine needed him now as never before. Napoleon had tolerated *Delphine*, but for how long? He could scarcely forgive her reference to the silence of France. Nor could he welcome her enthusiasm for the Calvinism of Lebensei. The First Consul had chosen to make his peace with Rome, and he could not help knowing that she had shut herself up in her town house on the day the Concordat was proclaimed, ignoring not only the grand procession to Notre Dame but the music which brought the triumph to a climax. Two orchestras of 150 men each, one led by Méhul, the other by Cherubini, had accompanied the hymns in the ruler's honor.

Finally Napoleon was bound to resent Germaine's

admiration of all things English. Appointed First Consul for life by a plebiscite that pledged nothing short of adoration, he was prepared for the elimination of the British Empire. In the spring of 1803 he insulted the British ambassador Lord Whitworth and broke the fragile peace of Amiens. A little while and the Duc d'Enghien would be murdered. A little while and the First Consul would be crowned Emperor by Pius VII. Dedicated to the humiliation of the enemy across the Channel, he demanded absolute obedience.

"He stands in fear of me," Germaine bravely believed. "That is my joy, that is my pride, and that is my terror." Daringly she set out in the fall of 1803 from Geneva, settling at Maffliers, ten leagues from Paris. It was there she learned that gendarmes were on the road to order her far from the capital. Thinking that Napoleon *might* have relented, she made her way to Madame Récamier's residence at Saint-Brice, which was only two leagues out from Paris. While she was dining, a man in a gray suit rang at the door. He explained that he came from the gendarmerie of Versailles, but had put on civilian clothes so as not to disturb her unduly. His orders were final: she must move to a point no less than forty leagues distant from Paris.

"You see where it all ends," Germaine told the officer, "if a woman has a mind of her own. I'd advise you to warn every woman in your family."

Hoping against hope, Germaine pushed on to Paris. There a gendarme called every day at her town house, urging her to leave. She wrote to Joseph Bonaparte, trusting that he might take an interest in the education of her older son. "One of the great misfortunes of persecution," she said, "is that one has to beg for the very air one breathes. . . . I must know where I can spend the winter. If I can't stay in Paris, I must have a passport to take my son to some German university, and I can't wait to make up my mind, for the roads may become impossible at any moment. I should have preferred to send my son to the Ecole Polytechnique instead of having to give him a foreign education. But can I stand any longer the unjust treatment I'm receiving?"

"I've heard from you," Joseph answered. "I went out this morning on purpose to Saint-Cloud, and I have done everything which you might expect, knowing how I feel, but I don't believe I've been successful."

Germaine appealed to Napoleon himself. "I was," she wrote, "living at Peace in Maffliers on the understanding you gave me that I could stay on there, when I was told that gendarmes were on their way to seize me and my children. Citizen Consul, I could not believe that you could give me such a cruel place in history.

"You are breaking the heart of my respected father who, in spite of his age, would like to ask you what crime either I or any member of my family has committed to deserve such barbarous treatment. If you want me to leave France, give me a passport for Germany. . . .

"Citizen Consul, I cannot believe that you are willing to persecute a woman and her children. A hero is obliged to protect the weak. I beg you once again, grant me your complete forgiveness, let me live at Saint-Ouen. It's near enough Paris for my son to enter the Ecole Polytechnique at the right time, and far enough away so that I won't have any home in Paris.

"I'll go away in the spring, when traveling will be easier for my children.

"Finally, Citizen Consul, you would do well to spend a minute or two in reflection before bringing so much grief on the head of a defenseless person. By an act of simple justice, you can win my gratitude, which will be more lasting than you can imagine."

There was no answer, but a passport was provided for Germany.

On the 19th of October, 1803, Germaine set out from Paris with her children. With Benjamin at her side, and with Napoleon's oblique blessing, she was about to enjoy the great adventure of her life.

CHAPTER NINE

THE CROSSING
OF THE RHINE

———◆———

T H E R E was a time when Germaine fancied that learning German was as odd an occupation as packing one's trunks for a journey one would never undertake. In the spring of 1796 she had the opportunity of meeting Wieland in Zurich, but she saw no sense in taking the trouble, even though the creator of *Oberon* was something of a celebrity. "To go to Zurich to see a German author, no matter how famous he may be, that's something I shan't be guilty of. I believe I already know as well as any German what the Germans are up to, and even what they'll be up to fifty years from now. I'm sure they have talent, but I can't say they're clever, and in conversation wit is the only thing that counts."

It was true that she had sent Goethe and Schiller copies of her essay on the *Influence of Passion*, but she had done so out of courtesy rather than out of eagerness to brave the authors face to face. Of course she could not resent the fact that Goethe had gone so far as to translate a shorter piece of hers on imaginative literature. This was published in *Die Horen*, the review that he and Schiller founded.

Goethe was also so amiable as to forward a copy of *Wilhelm Meisters Lehrjahre*, but Germaine was not overcome by the honor. She admitted that the binding was superb; however, "as it was written in German, all I could do was admire the binding. . . . Confidentially," she told a friend, "Benjamin informs me that I'm better off than he is, and he has read the book."

But Germaine discovered that she could not remain indifferent. In the spring of 1799 she could not help sending Goethe the manuscript of *De la littérature.* "In the chapter on German literature," she wrote him, "you'll find that I've tried to express my appreciation. I must sing your praises whenever I write, for of all your admirers, there is no one, I'm sure, who has more enthusiasm for your work than I have. Reading *Werther* was one of the great experiences of my life. *La nouvelle Héloïse* is a masterpiece, but so is *Werther.* So that I might be better prepared to comprehend your achievement, I began studying German two months ago. I must read you in your own language." By the following year she was well on the way to mastering even the grammar.

She was not wasting her time. Although no one could pretend that the Germans matched the admirable performance, century after century, of the French, their legacy was rich, so rich that it was only imperfectly comprehended at the dawn of the nineteenth century. Even if the Germans had no medieval historians to compare with Joinville, they had produced poets and mystics who were gallant representatives of the age of Saint Louis on the other side of the Rhine. The *Nibelungenlied* may be more legend than poetry, but no such careless comment could be passed on the work of Walter von der Vogelweide, nor on the *Tristan und Isolde* of Gottfried von Strassburg, nor on the *Parsifal* of Wolfram von Eschenbach. As for Mechtild von Magdeburg, who composed *The Flowing Light of Godhood* in a thirteenth-century nunnery, she was much more than a name to Dante when he came to the *Divine Comedy*. Dante could scarcely forget her; she knew that the soul that died of love was buried in God.

So Goethe did not invent the German language, in spite of the brave belief of the English-speaking world that German literature dates from the publication of *Werthers Leiden*. The influence of Martin Luther's Bible was comparable to that of the King James Version, and in the seventeenth century not even the anarchy of the Thirty Years' War silenced the baroque poets led by Paul Gerhardt.

The literature was reborn in the late eighteenth century, and the accomplishments of Lessing, Goethe, and Schiller could not be ignored for long. There were Germanists whose native tongue was French. One of the most enthusiastic of these was a certain Charles de Villers, a captain of the Royal Company of Artillery, who fled to Göttingen in 1794 when the cause of the Bourbons proved hopeless. Villers was as loyal to his second home as he had been to Louis XVI; in fact, Kant himself might have been embarrassed by the eagerness with which this disciple devoured the *Critique of Pure Reason*. Villers was annoyed when Germaine hinted to him in 1802 that she doubted such a thing as taste was prevalent across the Rhine.

"Madame," he enlightened the author of *Delphine*. "I live in the midst of the leaders of German literature . . . whom you accuse of lacking taste. Allow me to tell you quite frankly that German men of letters are quite superior to what passes for *taste* in France. That shabby old deity of our boudoirs, with her fragile bow and arrows, her hoop skirts, and her wig *à la Louis XIV*, is not worthy of taking a seat in the picturesque

Parnassus of Germania. Long, long ago, a good kick
from the Teutonic muse sent her flying into the mud
puddles. . . . The Teutonic muse holds in her hands
a lyre of sturdy oak, her blond tresses, decked with
mistletoe, flutter in the breeze; her only garment is an
ethereal bit of drapery. If some god of taste should
pursue her in her flight, you may be sure he won't be
wearing silk stockings and red heels."

Germaine was not quite convinced, but Villers was
not discouraged. "My only ambition," he wrote her, "is
to tell the truth, and my only fault is that I've told only
half the truth up to now." He absorbed *Delphine* and
he went on to remind the author that "only since Voltaire's time has justice been done in France to the admirable literature of the English. All that is needed
now is for a genius to be inspired by the profound origi-
nality of certain German writers, and then the French
will understand that the Germans have not only revealed the most profound thoughts, but have also expressed the emotions with a new energy."

At that very moment Villers was laying the ground-
work for his treatise on *The essentially different manner in which French and German poets treat the subject of love.* "Charming words like *Sehnsucht, Ahnung,*
and *Schwärmerei,*" he said with a sigh, "don't even
exist in the vocabulary of the French poets! And one
can't invent words for feelings one has never experienced."

Germaine was willing to believe that "the intellect
of mankind" was temporarily residing in Germany, but
she was puzzled rather than pleased when Villers informed her that "the Germans are fundamentally kind,
benevolent, and hospitable in the noblest sense of the
word. Unlike the Parisians, they have not refined the
arts of enjoyment. They can't pretend to show off all
the graces, nor do they have those elegant manners to

which you attach so much importance. But they are natural, they are calm, and they are good." He was in Paris for the moment, and he was disgusted. "If I were condemned to spend the rest of my life here, I couldn't bear the thought."

"Monsieur," Germaine replied, "there is a bitterness in your letter which makes me feel that our meeting in Metz may have been a mistake. Your letters bore no trace of this before we met, and if you think it over, you may realize that the way you've been acting doesn't give one a pleasant idea of either the French or the Germans."

In her diary Germaine made plain that Napoleon could never eradicate her love of France. "I've always thought," she wrote, "that hatred, even when I was the victim, was nothing but an extraordinary accident. . . . When I come across an enemy, I'm tempted to ask him: *Are you really serious about hating me?*"

As for Germany, she was still beset by doubts. "I must confess," she wrote to Villers as she drew near the border, "that the outward appearance of Germany is not very aesthetic. Every voice, every accent, every mannerism tells me that France is disappearing, and you, too, you who have built a bridge between our good manners and the good points of our neighbors. I fear I shan't find anyone like you across the Rhine."

Villers's only answer was to complain that she was unfair to the prose of Jean-Paul Richter. "All of nature," he reminded her, "cannot be contained in a garden by Le Nôtre. You can tell nothing about the morals of a nation by talking to one or two people. In France people exist only for Paris, and in Paris only for three or four closed circles. In Germany people work for the nation as a whole, even to the extent of making sacrifices for those who live in the little towns and villages."

All this may have been true, but Germaine was depressed when she reached Frankfurt am Main in the middle of November. "I haven't yet been separated from Benjamin," she wrote her father, "so that the awful leaden weight of Germany has not yet fallen upon me. He has showed himself to no one; I keep him with me in my hotel like a prisoner. . . . Frankfurt is a city without any intellectual pretensions, and as far as the practical side of life is concerned, Germany is unbearable."

There were moments when Germaine thought she had committed the blunder of her life. "I shudder," she told Necker, "when I think of the four months' trip I've set out on. I don't imagine I'll suffer any real inconvenience, people seem to be very pleasant, the newspapers have said nothing unkind, and the curiosity I arouse is evident, but I'll know I'm in prison as soon as Benjamin leaves me. It is really impossible to live anywhere except in one's own country."

She could not begin to conceal her reactions from Villers. "Shall I," she wrote him from Frankfurt, "give you my impressions, like a real Frenchwoman, of a country I've spent only a couple of days in, and don't yet know? I've already listened to someone torturing a piano in the smoky public room of an inn, with woolen clothes put out to dry on the oven. That's the way everything seems to me: a concert in a smoke-filled room, all the poetical feeling you could ask for, but none of the outward graces."

She was no better pleased by Gotha. "There is," she informed Necker, "nothing in the world that's heavier or more stupefying in the moral and physical sense than the average German. I can't speak about the women, but up to the present moment I can't see how they can fall in love with anything except ideals, for you can't imagine anyone more matter-of-fact than the men they have to marry." But this was only the beginning of her indictment. "There's something Gothic about German customs, even if there is something of the eighteenth century about their ideas. Mediocre men are more mediocre here than anywhere else."

She called on Friedrich Melchior Baron von Grimm, who had known Diderot and Rousseau, but even he was a disappointment. "All his defects are exaggerated by the fact that he is eighty years old. He's clumsy, he's slow-witted, he makes dull jokes, he's as witless as the most stupid aristocrat." She was equally displeased by the Hereditary Prince of Gotha. "He puts on rouge," she told Necker. "He may have a daring idea or two in his head, but he's a man of effeminate tastes."

Germaine's only consolation was the sound of the aeolian harps she kept hearing in the gardens of the German noblemen. She bought one for her father and sent it on to Coppet. To Necker she admitted that she had thought more than once of heading for Geneva. "But they've been saying in Paris that I wouldn't dare go to Germany, for fear I wouldn't be well received, and that makes it impossible for me to turn back." She pushed on to Weimar, which she reached by the middle of December.

Weimar was a sensible destination. Although the Grand Duke Karl August* was not one of the brilliant rulers of the eighteenth century, he was a pleasant representative of the Enlightenment, and he had an eye for talent. His education had been supervised by Wieland, who settled in Weimar for the rest of his life. But Wieland was only one of several poets in residence. Goethe had come as early as 1775, and the Grand Duke had found his advice invaluable on agriculture, on horticulture, and on mining. Herder, who died in the week of Germaine's arrival, had come in 1776 and been ap-

* To be precise, he was merely a duke in 1803; he was not elevated to grand duke until 1815.

112

pointed court preacher at Goethe's suggestion. Finally, Schiller had come in 1799, to be still another retainer.

The cast at Weimar was impressive but it was not complete. No one ruler could hope to capture all of the great writers of the age; talent, even genius, was more plentiful than in the days of Walter von der Vogelweide. Then, too, every writer was not intended to entertain the aristocracy; no court could detain a poet who believed in total commitment to his work. Novalis, Hölderlin, and Kleist, whose passionate dedication could be compared only to that of Baudelaire, Rimbaud, and Lautréamont in nineteenth-century France, did not figure on the Grand Duke's list of appointments.

Friedrich Leopold Baron von Hardenberg, to give Novalis his real name, was for a time the auditor of a salt works, but he was not meant for this world. Not yet twenty-nine when he died of consumption in 1801, he lived, like the hero of his novel *Heinrich von Ofterdingen*, for the quest of the blue flower. "Evening has come while I was glancing at the dawn," he wrote on the third day after the death of the fifteen-year-old girl who was to have been his bride. "Evening has come, and I have a premonition that I shall die young." There was nothing morbid about his yearning for death, which was satisfied four years later. Nor was there a trace of affectation in the slender volume of his collected works. Merciless with himself, he was provoked by the matter-of-fact pages he came across in *Wilhelm Meister*. "Goethe," he damned the great man, "has done for German poetry what Wedgwood has done for English art." *Prosaic* is an adjective that has never been applied to Novalis's *Hymns to the Night*.

Johann Christian Friedrich Hölderlin wandered for the last thirty-seven years of his life in the night of insanity, occasionally baring the extent of his despair by ripping the strings out of a piano. In his sane years he succeeded in shattering almost every comfortable tradition of German poetry. He was not, however, really appreciated until the twentieth century, when Rainer Maria Rilke was moved (perhaps by his example) to compose the *Duino Elegies*. Hölderlin was encouraged by Schiller, but not by Goethe, who carelessly thumbed through the novel *Hyperion* in the author's presence without once giving him a glance. In fact, Goethe was so far from comprehending Hölderlin's mission that he advised him to stick to poetry "with human interest in it."

Another poet who paid the price of madness was Bernd Heinrich Wilhelm von Kleist. On the 21st of November, 1811, he and Frau Henriette Vogel, a young woman who was incurably diseased and with whom he was apparently in love, strolled to the banks of the Sacred Lake near Potsdam. They had indulged in a number of bottles of wine and rum and had drunk sixteen cups of coffee. He then took a loaded pistol and shot her through the heart. She fell dead; he reloaded the pistol and killed himself. Her husband, commented the London *Time*s a week or two later, "has been blamed for giving *éclat* to a catastrophe over which it would have been better to draw the thickest veil."

"I could never think of this poet," Goethe remarked, "without shuddering." He was not referring to Kleist's awful end; he was discussing Kleist's work. Was he embarrassed by the perfection of the suicide's prose? The glacial elegance of a tale like *The Marquise d'O.* may never be surpassed. Or was he baffled by the fury of the heroine of *Penthesilea?* This may have been the case. "She comes of such a strange race, and lives in such a strange world that I must take a little time to get accustomed to her," he wrote the author after sampling the drama. "You must also allow me to say (for if one can't be forthright, one might as well keep silence) that I am always disturbed and worried, when I see young men of intellect and talent look forward to the theater of the future. A Jew expecting the Messiah, a Christian expecting the New Jerusalem, or a Portuguese expecting Don Sebastian,* can't make me feel more uneasy."

But it would be unfair to think of Goethe merely as the man who overlooked or misjudged Novalis, Hölderlin, and Kleist. Germaine had made up her mind to see him, and her ambition was far from foolish. "The greater the man," Goethe conceded, "the more likely he is to fall under the influence of the daemonic, and he must watch out that his own will be done." On another occasion he defined the daemonic "as that which cannot be analyzed by the intellect. There is nothing daemonic in my nature, but I can be easily enslaved."

The riddle of Goethe, like the riddle of Thomas Jefferson, will never be explained. Like Jefferson in the political world, Goethe won almost limitless admiration for the apparent serenity with which he went from one triumph to another. If he had cared, he could have rivaled Novalis in the exploration of dreams: he made that plain in his uncanny *Fairy Tale*. He also understood the yearning for the ancient world that led Hölderlin to write *Hyperion*. His own *Iphigenie auf Tauris* is the only modern drama of classic inspiration that may be placed next to the best of Racine. Finally, there were times when he came close to excusing the fury that forced Kleist to a theme like *Penthesilea*. "We should only grow older," he said, "in order to be more understanding. I can think of no weakness of which I could not be guilty myself." He had his mediocre moments, as Novalis testified. But his mediocre moments may be forgiven; by the end of 1803, when Germaine appeared

* The sixteenth-century king whose death was doubted by his followers. *Dom*, not *Don* is proper in Portuguese.

in Weimar, he had already proved he was the greatest virtuoso of the age.

Faust I was not yet in print, but he had moved far beyond *Götz von Berlichingen*, the romantic drama with which he had launched his career in 1771. At fifty-four he had come to believe that to be romantic was to be obvious, and he was repenting the reputation he had acquired with *Werther* twenty-nine years before. *Iphigenie*, *Tasso*, and *The Italian Journey* (the record of two years' traveling in the peninsula) told of his desire to impose a neoclassic trend. *The Roman Elegies* proved that, to this neoclassic, poetry was the memory of passion spent. He had also, and this must not be forgotten, reminded the scientific world that the human jawbone betrayed traces of something similar to the intermaxillary bone of the ape. Like so many other representatives of the Enlightenment, he had an incorrigible interest in science. The time would come when he would spend hour after hour satisfying himself (if not other scientists) that Newton's color theory was indefensible.

Goethe had never *fallen* in love; he never would. He could be passionate, but he could never take any woman seriously. His magnificent mother, who spelled humor and wisdom when he was a little boy in Frankfurt, left, so it seemed, an indelible impression. Again and again he was charmed by women. He was delighted, for example, by Friedrike Brion, the Alsatian pastor's daughter whom he described in his autobiography. But he was never caught, not even by Charlotte von Stein, the sensitive intellectual who was married to the Grand Duke's Master of the Stables. He was close to her before the Italian journey, but never again. Apparently he was comfortable only with his mistress Christiane Vulpius, an uneducated girl whom he put in charge of his Weimar residence in 1788. She bore him a son, but he waited eighteen years to marry her.

"I have never met a more presumptuous man than I am," Goethe admitted, "and the fact that I say so means that what I am saying is the truth. I never believed in *trying* to do anything. Whatever I set out to do, I found I had already accomplished." This supreme facility, which was obvious to everyone with whom Goethe came in contact, was occasionally discouraging to other authors. It meant, as Friedrich Schiller understood at their first meeting, that he needed no one in whom to confide.

"To see Goethe very often," Schiller told a friend in 1789, "would make me an unhappy man. Even with his closest friends he never lets himself go. He simply can't be got hold of. I believe, to tell you the truth, that he is an extreme egotist. He has just what it takes to control other people, and to make himself agreeable doing favors of one sort or another, but he knows how to maintain his own independence. He spreads his benevolence far and wide, but like a god, without once surrendering himself. . . .

"No one in his right mind," Schiller decided, "should allow such a creature in his presence. I detest him thoroughly, even though I love his intellect with all my heart and expect great things of him. . . . I find he has aroused in me a curious blend of hatred and love, a feeling not unlike that which Brutus and Cassius must have had for Caesar. I could murder him for his brains, and still love him with all my heart."

Schiller lived to revise this opinion, although he must have resented to the end the security that was Goethe's birthright as the grandson of the mayor of Frankfurt. His own life was troubled enough. The son of an army surgeon who had a real reverence for the rights enjoyed by the British people, he was bullied as a boy by Duke Karl Eugen of Württemberg. The Duke saw to his education in military school and later had him trained to be a physician, but had no intention of tolerating a poet. Schiller had to steal away from Stuttgart to watch the first performance of his first drama *Die Räuber* in Mannheim. He stole off to Mannheim once again; on his return he was discovered and put under a fortnight's arrest with the warning that he was to write no more "comedies" and to communicate with no one beyond the borders of Württemberg. This was more than he could bear. Schiller escaped to freedom and to the painful fact that a dramatist in Germany could not expect to earn a good living from the box office.

If it had not been for the kindness of Christian Gottfried Körner, who sheltered him in Leipzig and Dresden, and of two Danish noblemen, who provided him with a pension for three years, Schiller might have foundered. In the end he owed his security to Goethe. For it was Goethe who got him a job teaching history at Jena in 1789, and without Goethe's influence he might never have reached the haven of Weimar ten years later.

At his very first glimpse of Weimar in 1787, Schiller understood that this community of barely 6,000 people offered all that he wished for. The houses were "so many snail shells out of which the inhabitants seldom stirred, even for a snatch of sunlight. . . . Weimar," he decided, "is paradise on earth. Everyone lives his own life, without attracting any special attention. Whatever government there is, is hardly noticeable; its only function is to allow everyone to enjoy peace, air, and sunlight. But if you are looking for companionship, or want to make your way in the world or show off your intelligence, that too is possible."

There remained, of course, the Goethe problem, which could not be solved overnight. "That man is standing in my way," Schiller reflected, "and he reminds me all too often that fate has dealt me a rough deal." Körner had told him that the great man spent his odd moments fondling plants and stones, and to Schiller, who was not a professional naturalist, this may have seemed an atrocious waste of time.

Schiller was also disturbed by what he heard of Goethe's home life. "He's beginning to get on in years," he informed Körner in 1790, "and his scandalous interest in the female sex seems to be catching up with him. The girl in his life is a certain Mamsell Vulpius, who has got a child by him." This was the very year in which Schiller married Charlotte von Lengefeld, the daughter of the Chief Forester of the Black Forest. The poet was not, it must be admitted, the most imaginative man where women were concerned. He invited his wife's sister to live with him and his bride, never guessing that he was courting friction.

But Schiller was a man of startling intuitions, even if he could not condone Goethe's keeping a mistress. This aspect of his character was apparent in July, 1794, when he and Christiane's lover happened to be on hand for a meeting of a society of naturalists in Jena. "By chance we fell into conversation afterwards," Goethe recalled. "He seemed to have taken a certain interest in the proceedings, but he pointed out to me, showing an uncommon penetration for which I was more than grateful, that such a specialized approach to the natural sciences could never attract the layman who might otherwise play a real part.

"To which," said Goethe, "I answered that nature is perhaps a riddle to naturalists themselves, and that there might well be another way of attacking the problem. Nature might be examined, not in its minute particulars, but as an active, living organism. He was willing to be convinced, but he had his doubts. He could not conceive that what I was talking about might be discovered by the process of deduction.

E

"We reached his lodgings," Goethe went on, "and our conversation became more and more animated. I then entered into an earnest discussion of the metamorphosis of plants, and with a few strokes of the pen conjured up a symbolic plant for his instruction. He showed a real interest in what I was saying, and took everything in with a singular power of comprehension. But when I'd come to the end, he shook his head. *That is not a deduction*, he said. *That is an idea.*

"I was taken by surprise," Goethe admitted. "I was even annoyed. . . . I was on the verge of losing my temper, but I controlled myself and answered: *It is quite possible that I enjoy having ideas without knowing that they are ideas.*"

Schiller's hour had struck. Goethe had at last met a man with whom he could carry on an argument. From this moment their friendship was indestructible, even though Goethe, whose sense of smell made it impossible for him to touch a dish flavored with garlic, was made most uncomfortable by the scent of the moldering apples which Schiller, for some reason of his own, kept stuffing into bureau drawers.

"You must not expect any great wealth of ideas from me," Schiller warned his new friend. "That's precisely what I'll expect from you. What I need and what I am striving for is to make a great deal out of very little, and when you come to realize the deficiencies of my intellectual equipment, you may have to confess I haven't done badly.

"You have a particularly intuitive mind," he continued, "and all your mental powers seem to be centered on the imagination. . . . As a matter of fact, this is the highest achievement of which a man is capable—as long as he is successful in generalizing his perceptions, and his instincts are authoritative."

Schiller's own aim, he reminded Goethe, was to be a

symbolist, and he feared that the poet in himself was often at war with the philosopher. "Even at the present time," he conceded, "my imagination may wreck the fabric of my abstractions, and my intellect may harm my poetry. If only I can be the master of both, granting each certain specified liberties!"

Here Schiller was too modest. Although the dignity of man has become an all too familiar slogan in the twentieth century, having been used once too often in graduation addresses, there is no doubt whatever that he succeeded better than any modern playwright in dramatizing the importance of human rights. Until the dust settles on the Declaration of Independence and the Declaration of the Rights of Man, Schiller's dramas will command their audience.

By the time Germaine drew near Weimar, he had turned forty-four, and was tired of the anarchistic gospel he had preached with such startling success in *Die Räuber*. As early as 1787 he had produced *Don Carlos*, and with the Marquis Posa's cry for freedom of thought, completely deserved the honorary citizenship he was given by the revolutionary government of France. For a moment he was tempted to travel to Paris, but the execution of Louis XVI made him realize that the most glorious ideals could be sacrificed for expediency. Divorcing himself from politics, he dedicated himself to exploring the conflicts of conscience in kings and queens, statesmen and soldiers. By 1799 he had completed the tragedy of *Wallenstein;* by 1800, *Maria Stuart;* and by 1801, *Die Jungfrau von Orleans.*

He was at work on *Wilhelm Tell* when the news reached him that Germaine had crossed the Rhine, and he was understandably alarmed. He had never met a woman of her powers, and he was not sure he would enjoy the challenge. "Madame de Staël is already in Frankfurt," he wrote Goethe on November 30, 1803, "and we may expect her here at any moment. If only she understands German, I am confident that we can get the better of her, but if we have to listen to our creed being recited in French, and with typical French glibness, I fear it may be too much for us."

Goethe, who found himself in Jena on the date of Germaine's arrival in Weimar, was at first inclined to share Schiller's misgivings. "It was to be expected," he wrote Schiller, "that I'd be called back to Weimar as soon as Madame de Staël drew near. I've been thinking things over, for I don't want to be upset, and I've decided I should remain here. In this unpleasant time of year, I've just enough physical strength to survive."

Goethe's mother feared the worst. She knew that her son had never taken any woman seriously, and she was not sure the experience would be beneficial. "Madame de Staël is now in Weimar, I hear," she noted. "She made an unmistakable impression on me; it was just like having a millstone around my neck. I kept out of her way, avoided every gathering to which she was invited, and drew a deep breath as soon as she was gone. What on earth could that woman see in me? I've never in my life written so much as a spelling book, and I hope that my good angel will save me from doing any such thing in the future."

But Goethe was determined to be polite. From Jena he wrote Germaine a letter in the French language. "I find myself," he said, "in a strange position. There you are in Weimar, and I am not rushing this minute to extend you the assurance of my complete devotion. However, I shan't complain of the business which keeps me here for the moment, nor of my physical indisposition. These are accidents which are dear to me, for they allow me to hope for a pleasure which I should not have presumed to wish for. You are drawing near a hermit, a hermit who will do all he can to cast aside any cares which might prevent him from dedicating himself completely to making you feel at home. You will light up these sad days for me, and the long nights will seem as short as so many seconds. . . ."

This was perhaps more than Schiller deemed necessary. He had already written Goethe that he understood his reasons for not dashing off to Weimar, and he had tried to explain matters to the Grand Duke. It would certainly be wiser for Goethe to have Madame de Staël to himself. "It will be much more pleasant for her to see you without any distraction," he pointed out, "and the meeting may even be a pleasant occasion for you, instead of being a burden impossible to bear."

Germaine indicated that she was willing to travel to Jena for Goethe's sake, but this was an honor that Goethe declined. "No, Madam," he wrote her from Jena on December 19, "I can't think of your making that short but disagreeable journey in all this snow. On Saturday I shall be at your service, and I hope that you will come to dine at my house with Monsieur and Madame Schiller. Madame, I grow more and more impatient to see you every day, and you would be well satisfied with your old friend if only you could read my mind. . . . Don't forget that these days were set aside for you; I'd have made the trip on Monday in your carriage, only I didn't want to think of wasting a single one of these precious moments."

There is no doubt that Germaine was impatient to meet Goethe and Schiller; there is also no doubt that her impatience was mixed with irreverence. "Goethe and Schiller," she had written Necker on the 15th, "have their heads stuffed with the craziest metaphysics that you can imagine, and as they live all by themselves and are much admired, they go on thinking their own thoughts, and are taken terribly seriously. It's very easy to satisfy a German audience, and from that standpoint, you mustn't be impressed by my triumphs, for a public that is easily satisfied will be the ruin of any author."

Schiller was the first to survey the phenomenon that was Germaine; he wrote Goethe on the 21st that she was worth the trip. "She is all of one piece," he told the Grand Duke's favorite, "and there isn't any single false note or pathological trait in her nature. All this means that one can get along with her quite easily, in spite of the vast difference between her way of thinking and ours, and that one can afford to listen to what she has to say. She stands for French culture in all of its simplicity, and she casts an interesting light on the subject. As far as philosophy is concerned, particularly in the noblest sense of the word, we'll never understand each other, no matter how long the conversation lasts. But her instincts are better than her metaphysics, and her intellect, which is first-rate, is capable of rising to certain heights. She wants to explain everything, she wants to examine everything, and she wants to pass judgment on everything. She can't conceive of any dark or intangible forces, and what she can't light up with her torch might just as well not exist. For this very reason she has a genuine dislike of the philosophy of idealism, which in her opinion can lead only to mysticism and superstition, and that is one of her limitations."

Would Germaine ever appreciate poetry? Schiller was of the opinion that poetry was beyond her. "But she can't bear a false note," he told Goethe. "It's sad that she can't recognize what we know to be the truth. You can see from what I have been saying that the clarity of her mind, her outspoken manner, and her intellectual vivacity will not displease you. The only unfortunate thing is the nimbleness of her tongue. I don't make out too well, since I'm none too proficient in speaking French, but you, with all the practice you've had, will find it easy to communicate with her.

"My advice," Schiller continued, "would be for you to come over on Saturday, make her acquaintance, and then return to finish your business in Jena. If Madame de Staël stays after the New Year, you can always find her here, and if she leaves earlier than that, she can always visit you in Jena. The important thing is for you to lose no time in getting an idea of what she's like, and put an end to the tension you must be under."

Germaine has left her own account of her discussions with Schiller. "I warmly defended," she wrote, "the superiority of the French drama over that of all other nations. He could not refuse the opportunity of entering into an argument with me, and without thinking for a second of how hard it was for him to express himself in French, paying no attention to the opinions of the other people in the room (who were not on his side), began to confess his heartfelt convictions. In the beginning I used French weapons to refute him; I was amusing, and I was vivacious. But very shortly I made out from what Schiller was saying that he had a good many ideas, even if he didn't know the French for them. I was also struck by the simplicity of his character, a simplicity which forced this genius into a struggle in which he couldn't find the words to express himself. I found he was so modest about his own success, and so compelling when he was defending what he belived to be the truth, that I could not help admiring the man."

"Didn't I do well?" Germaine asked Schiller's wife. "How sad I am that I can't speak Schiller's language! But you are a delightful interpreter of our thoughts."

Lotte Schiller had to admit she was rather fond of Germaine. "She's constantly on the go," she noted. "She wants to know everything, see everything, and try everything out. But no matter how earnest she may seem, she has a certain French superficiality about her, and I might add that she is a trifle too free in passing judgment. This last trait doesn't always appeal to us Germans, who would rather look on the bright side of things. However, she has no malice in her, and every word she says proves her noble love of the truth."

In the meantime Germaine let Goethe know that she was not to be taken for granted. "You won't be entertaining a Parisian," she informed him. "You will be entertaining the woman who has shed more tears than anyone else over Werther and Egmont."

This seems to have made an impression on Goethe. In the memorandum he transcribed after her departure he confessed he was sorry that he could enjoy only part of her stay in the proper "historical" manner. He was down with a very bad cold, and he had to keep to his own room for much of the time, saving himself for small gatherings.

More than once Germaine caught him off balance. "Although," he wrote, "I had no good reason to conceal my thoughts from her, something came up which made me quite shy for a moment or two. I had just received a new French book, containing the correspondence of two Frenchwomen with Rousseau. They had succeeded in completely mystifying that shy, inaccessible man, at first arousing his interest by doing him small favors, and then drawing him into writing letters which, after they had had enough of a joke, they collected and printed.

"I let Madame de Staël know that I disapproved of such proceedings, but she took it all very lightly; as a matter of fact she seemed to approve of what they had done, and gave me to understand in no uncertain manner that she was thinking of doing the same thing with us. Nothing more was needed to make me extremely circumspect."

There were times when Goethe believed that Germaine was overanxious to express *herself*. "She had several aims in view," he said. "She wished to come to grips with Weimar in the moral, social, and literary sense, and she wished to be correctly informed on all such matters. But she also wished to make herself known, and she was as eager to impose her ideas as she was to explore our mental processes. She could never leave well enough alone; she set out to make an impression on our senses, on our feelings, even on our minds; she wanted to rouse us to a certain activity, the lack of which she deplored."

Nor was this all. "As she had no understanding of the word *duty*, nor of the firm decisions made by men who live to do their duty, she insisted that as soon as she attacked, the field was to be cleared at once."

It was fortunate that Goethe had no opportunity of reading a letter that Germaine wrote the day after Christmas. "Goethe," she informed a friend of Villers, "is not Werther. He is getting fat—in parentheses, that's one of the German vices—and he isn't much to look at."

She was willing to admit that "in his slow way Goethe is a man of considerable intellect. Tell Villers he told me that *never in his life had he had a good time in Germany*. To tell you the truth, I'm the first person who has given the Germans an idea of what a good time is. They treat me as though I were a goddess, and I'm told they have never put themselves out for anyone the way they have for me."

Schiller was easier to digest, Germaine made plain. "He lives only for literature, like a geometrician for his projections, and he has never looked at things from the outside, but he is really very ingenious when you consider how serious he is."

She saw Goethe again and again, but never abandoned her reservations about the man, no matter how deeply she admired certain of his works. "Without any question," she admitted to Necker early in February, "the most interesting man here is Werther-Goethe. But he has a notion of his own importance which is equaled only by the weirdness of his imagination. He believes he is inspired by supernatural forces. . . . He believes that the universe, both ideally and concretely, is nothing but an idea, which is God, and he believes that he is closer to that idea than any man alive." Worst of all, she could never tell, when talking to him, just when she might have to attack his religion.

For his part Goethe wondered whether Germaine was wise in trying to win new laurels reciting in public. "I excused myself one evening, when she was giving *Phèdre*," he recalled. "The polite applause of the German audience did not quite satisfy her."

Her greatest mistake, Goethe believed, was "philosophizing in public, which is another word for showing off by discussing unsolvable problems." He found that she was inclined to bring up subjects better left between the individual and Almighty God. Worse yet, "as a woman and as a Frenchwoman, she insisted on being very positive on important points, and on not quite hearing what the other person was saying."

Goethe admitted that she aroused his evil genius. "Very often," he said, "I had to contradict her at every point, and I had to drive her to distraction, even though she had begun by being really polite and showed a certain brilliance in answering my questions."

There came one evening when Germaine felt she must shake him out of his lethargy. Striding into the room, she gave him the latest news about one of Napoleon's generals. "I have an important announcement to give you," she said. "Moreau and several others have been arrested and accused of treason against the tyrant."

"For some time," Goethe wrote in his account of this

incident, "I had, like everyone else, followed the achievements of the noble individual in question and I was well acquainted with all that he had done. In my quiet way I collected my thoughts and began to ponder the present before trying to guess the future. Whereupon the lady changed the subject, and started bringing up one indifferent topic after another. When she saw that I was lost in meditation and gave no sign of breaking into her conversation, she complained, as she had on previous occasions, that I was sulking and that there was no chance of getting a word out of me.

"At this point," Goethe recalled, "I became really angry. I told her that she was incapable of reaching any valid judgment. She had rushed into my house, given me a great shock, and then asked me to jump like a grasshopper from one subject to another."

Another evening, when Germaine and Goethe were dining with the Dowager Grand Duchess, he was once again exasperated. She was put out, as she often was, by the silence of the great man, and she dared to say that "I can only get on with Goethe when he has a bottle of champagne in him." This was too much. "I gather," Goethe muttered under his breath, "that we must have got drunk quite often together." Everyone began to laugh, and Germaine began to wonder why. Finally Benjamin succeeded in rendering a polite translation of the German.

But Goethe could not condemn Germaine. "Whatever one may think of the events I have been describing," he wrote, "we must realize that she was a woman of tremendous influence. She drove a breach in the Chinese wall of prejudices that separated us from France, so that we grew to be appreciated not only across the Rhine, but even across the English Channel. I think," he decided, "that we should look upon all the inconveniences we were put to as a blessing, even if the conflict of national characteristics did not seem beneficial at the time."

He also confessed he was thankful for the presence of Benjamin Constant, which was generous of him, for he and Germaine's great friend did not always see eye to eye. "I dined today with Goethe," wrote Benjamin in his diary for January 27, 1804, "and I feel that a Frenchman, even if he doesn't approve of all that is going on in his own country, is bound to be ill at ease with foreigners. I ran into no end of difficulties talking to Goethe. What a shame it is that he has fallen a victim to the spell of German mysticism! He admitted to me that it was all based on Spinozaism. Mystics on the order of Schelling do think very highly of Spinoza. But why on earth try to prove that he has anything to do with religion, let alone Catholicism? They say, it's because Catholicism is more poetic. *I'd rather be harmed by Catholicism*, Goethe told me, *than give up making use of it to make my plays more interesting.*"

Goethe was, of course, in no danger of becoming a Roman convert. He was simply indulging his taste for *mystification*, the very trait that led him more than once to disguise himself and take someone else's name before setting out on a journey. But Benjamin was concerned. "I am well acquainted," he said, "with Goethe's abuse of analogies, especially in this matter of his claims to know something about chemistry and the exact sciences."

Himself a moralist, Benjamin suspected that Goethe was amoral, at least as far as *Werther* was concerned. "What makes that book dangerous reading," *Werther*'s creator explained, "is that I described weakness as though it were strength. But when I do something that suits me, I am not at all interested in the consequences. If immature minds are injured reading what I write, so much the worse for them."

Benjamin dined once more with Goethe on the 16th of February. "He is a very bright man," he conceded. "He can be entertaining, he's not shallow, and he has a new idea or two. But he is the most unapproachable man I've ever met."

Unapproachable Goethe may have been, but Germaine and Benjamin found his society far more interesting that that of Wieland. The aging inventor of *Oberon* bent over backwards to be gracious, perhaps once too often. He saluted Germaine on her arrival by expressing regret that he was able to speak only his own language, "which unfortunately is the one in which Charles V talked to his horses." Germaine feared that he was too Frenchified to be useful. "It is I, Monsieur," she answered, "who must apologize for not understanding conversational German."

But Germaine was patient with Wieland. She was also patient with Henry Crabb Robinson, an underbred Englishman who was passing some time in Weimar in order to be thoroughly conversant with the latest manifestations of European culture. "You have not understood Goethe," Robinson presumed to enlighten her, "and you will never understand him." "Monsieur," Germaine answered, "I understand everything which deserves to be understood, and what I do not understand is nothing."

In the meantime she had come to certain conclusions. "The Germans," she wrote her father, "are an odd people who in their quiet way have a really romantic side. Unlike the French, they are far from sensitive. Unlike the Italians, they have no feelings to speak of. But they have succeeded in creating an ideal world of their own. . . . Exactly how one finds one's way into that world is a question I'm not prepared to answer."

Schiller, who had been wondering if Benjamin and Germaine would know when to leave, was pleasantly surprised on March 1 to learn that Constant was setting out for Switzerland and she for Berlin. "I feel," Schiller wrote Goethe, "as though I were recovering from a severe illness."

For once the creator of *Don Carlos* was unjust. Germaine had not come to Weimar to worship; she had come, as any journalist should, to inspect. She had made a thorough investigation, and she had made herself as agreeable as any journalist could. Frau von Stein, Goethe's early love, granted that "Madame de Staël is admired by everyone. For all her intellect, she is very benevolent." And the Grand Duke himself was so impressed that he handed Germaine a note of introduction to Queen Louise of Prussia.

It was on the 8th of March that she got to Berlin. Through the good offices of the Swedish ambassador's wife, she was presented at court and on the queen's birthday made her appearance at the state dinner and the ball that followed. "I hope, Madame," said the queen, "that you don't think we're so distinguished that we aren't flattered by your coming. I have admired you for many years, and I've been anxious to make your acquaintance."

But Berlin was not Weimar, even though Germaine was invited to be one of the 2,000 who attended a masked ball staged by Prince Henry of Prussia, with the prince himself playing the role of Alexander in a pageant depicting Alexander's marriage at Babylon to Statira, the widow of Darius. A little later, at still another ball, little Albertine gave a good cuff to the crown prince of Prussia. The king and queen expressed their displeasure over the incident by pointing out that the little girl had received a republican education. Albertine had to stay at home under house arrest for the next dance; but she was eventually forgiven by her royal hosts when she proved that the crown prince had slapped her first.

"I used to say when I was in Weimar," Germaine wrote Goethe's Dowager Grand Duchess, "that there was no point in putting up with the second-rate, and that German men were either exceedingly interesting or extremely dull. Mediocrity of that order is terribly obvious here; there are so many pretentious bores you would think you were back in Paris. I feel very far away from the tranquility of Weimar, where everyone knew his place."

"It seems very unlikely," the Dowager Grand Duchess admitted, "that anyone would find the graces of the Seine on that sandy soil."

Germaine also bared her discontent to Goethe. "This," she said, "is a country which does not appeal to the imagination. Society is drilled into a Prussian form, and the women must be surprised to find they are growing old, for they keep on saying and doing the same things for sixty years at a stretch, and time should stand still if one's mind is stationary. . . . If I settled in Germany, it certainly wouldn't be in a big city. Germans have no idea of how to make the most of city life."

But Berlin was not altogether disappointing. It was there, thanks to Goethe, that she met August Wilhelm von Schlegel.

Schlegel is a redoubtable name in the history of German literature, famed among other things for being the first to launch the study of Sanskrit. He was also responsible for a rather unnecessary essay comparing Racine's *Phèdre* to that of Euripides, to the former's disadvantage. He had, however, other accomplishments, and these should not be overlooked. He was a peerless translator of Shakespeare. And he was once a young man, younger than one would imagine from his prowess at Sanskrit.

The son of a Lutheran pastor, he had made his way to Göttingen, and after graduation had been a tutor in the family of a wealthy Englishman, later taking the same post in the home of a Dutch banker. On his return to Germany he had fallen in love with Karoline Böhmer, the twenty-seven-year-old widow of a country doctor. Karoline was an unpredictable person; she ran off to Mainz to stay with Professor Georg Forster and his clever wife Louise. Georg seems to have been eager rather than clever. He was such a passionate admirer of the French Revolution that he fled to Paris. Karoline was about to bear a child—father unknown—when she was clapped into prison by the invading French armies. On her release August Wilhelm was so gallant as to marry her. He was always fond of her, even after she divorced him to become the wife of the philosopher Schelling.

August Wilhelm could forgive Karoline almost anything. Schiller could never forgive her. She had fallen out of her chair laughing over "The Song of the Bell," one of Schiller's more ambitious poems, and he came to dread August Wilhelm and his younger brother Friedrich. As the editors of the *Athenaeum*, a review that challenged the supremacy of *Die Horen*, the brothers Schlegel and their close friend and collaborator Novalis championed the romantic movement, the very existence of which was a threat to Goethe's neoclassicism.

"Goethe," wrote Schiller in a melancholy mood, "has a weakness for the Schlegels." This may have been the case. The creator of *Faust* had never doubted himself. In recommending August Wilhelm to Germaine, he was displaying his wonted serenity, proving that he was not above doing a would-be rival a favor.

Germaine was delighted. "I've just met a man here," she wrote Necker on the 23rd of March, "who knows more about literature than anyone I can think of. . . . Benjamin can tell you that he enjoys a certain reputation in Germany, but what Benjamin doesn't know is that this man speaks French and English like a native, and that he has read everything, even though he's only thirty-six. I'm doing all I can to get him to come with me. He couldn't possibly tutor my children, he's too distinguished for that, but he could give Albert a few lessons in the months ahead, and that would be a great advantage to me for the book I have in mind." A week later, August Wilhelm von Schlegel joined her staff at a salary of 12,000 francs a year.

And then, on April 9, 1804, Necker died. Germaine was helpless in her grief.

Benjamin, who knew that she needed him and no one else, rushed to meet her at Weimar on her way back to Coppet. Earlier in the winter he had sensed that he and Germaine were closer than ever. "The only thing on earth that I respect is someone's sorrow," he had written his cousin, telling her of Germaine's anxieties away from France. "I want to die knowing that no one can accuse me of having looked the other way when someone was in misery."

Benjamin was not taken by August Wilhelm when he met him in Germaine's retinue at Weimar. "Schlegel," he wrote in his diary, "does his best to console her. He's clever and he is kind, but he has no real depth."

Nor did Benjamin understand why August Wilhelm, when they stopped at Würzburg, insisted on calling on Friedrich von Schelling. What was he, if not the seducer of Schlegel's wife? "Schlegel," Benjamin decided, "is one of the disciples, or better yet, one of the accomplices of Schelling. He knows a great deal about literature, he has a good mind, but he has next to no taste, and he is an odd sort of a show-off. Moreover, he has adopted such a weird terminology to describe the new German philosophy that it's next to impossible to understand what he is saying if one isn't already in the know. I believe, however, that I do understand him.

And if I'm not mistaken, his philosophical system is nothing but the subleties of scholasticism warmed over."

Benjamin was alarmed when August Wilhelm began expounding in the carriage on the beauties of the Middle Ages and the Roman Catholic Church. "Schlegel," he set down in his diary, "is certainly a believer in the strangest philosophy I've heard of. He yearns for a religion he doesn't believe in, and he thinks that one can re-establish a religion that has outlived its usefulness." Benjamin consoled himself with the thought that "Schlegel did not mean much to her."

At last, on the 19th of May, Germaine's carriage rolled into the courtyard of Coppet. "Our arrival in this abandoned château," Schlegel wrote his friend the Countess of Voss, "was the most terrifying moment of our trip. We had taken great pains to spend the night before in the neighborhood, so as to reach here early in the morning.

"All morning long," he went on, "she was sunk in the most somber silence. After we left Nyon she was terribly tense, in fact she was on the verge of convulsions. We had to keep her quiet every second in order to avoid a stroke." The valet kept urging the coachman on.

"The curtains were drawn, and I had to use physical force to keep them down, for every second of the way she wanted to raise them for a look at the château from far off. In the little town a number of people tried to press close to our carriage. When we drew up like a thunderclap in the courtyard of the château, she did not descend from the carriage, she fell out, and I have never heard a more ghastly shriek than hers, when she was borne off by her servants into the house."

Opiates were administered.

Later, when Germaine began to recover, her first thought was to read over her father's papers. She was sick with grief. But she would not have been Germaine if she had given up. She was only thirty-eight, too young to have grieving become her profession. Gradually she became aware that she had a mission. She would explain Germany to the world.

CHAPTER TEN

THE MISFORTUNES
OF CORINNE

———◆———

GERMAINE in the summer of 1804 was a woman
with a mission, but she was not a missionary. This was
apparent to Benjamin. When he came to write the novel
Cécile, he could not resist endowing the Madame de
Malbée of his fancy with many of the characteristics of
Madame de Staël. Like his great friend, Madame de
Malbée suffered the loss of her father. "Her grief,"
wrote Benjamin, "was sincere, but it bored her. So she
went off to Italy in search of distractions."

This was exactly what Germaine did, but she was
too independent to be predictable. Day after day the
lovers analyzed each other, dissecting their passion with
such care that even the wreck of their love—wrecked
it was, inevitably—was a work of architecture.

"Grief," Benjamin reflected on the road from Weimar
to Coppet, "is forever assailing mankind. There are two
approaches to dealing with this terrible enemy. You
may avoid grief as much as possible, escape from it
by distractions and pleasures of all kinds. Or you may
seize grief by the collar, fight it to the finish, and let

the struggle itself be your only distraction. I wonder if this second method isn't the better of the two."

This must not be taken as a criticism of Germaine. Kindness was one of Benjamin's faults. He proved this, as the summer wore on at Coppet, by his patience with August Wilhelm von Schlegel. He had noted, on the ride down from Germany, that August Wilhelm's eyes filled with tears when he emphasized the importance of Cervantes' contribution to literature. This was a bad sign, Benjamin decided. "His system has become such a personal thing that if you attack it he undergoes real physical suffering."

Matters were not improved when August Wilhelm's brother Friedrich arrived on the scene at the end of September. He was fat as a pumpkin, and although Benjamin admitted there was something charming about the man whenever he listened to anyone else, he did not listen too often. He was positively repulsive when he smiled; he was more like a servant than a house guest. His conversion to the Roman Catholic Church was four years in the future, but his leanings were evident. "His principles are as absurd as those of his brother," Benjamin set down in his diary.

"I can see now," he went on discussing the Schlegel brothers, "that their attitude toward life is a purely personal thing which they have gilded with the title of philosophy. They have come out in favor of Catholicism because the Protestant philosophers have made fun of them. They can't stand governments that allow freedom of the press because the presses have been used to attack them."

Friedrich went away in November, which was a blessing, since August Wilhelm by himself presented such a problem. To Benjamin he was a frightful coward and horribly self-centered. There came one long evening when August Wilhelm and Germaine laid down what seemed to be the rules of conversation. "Could any-thing be more mad than trying to educate a tutor?" Germaine's great friend reflected in his diary. "And how boring it is for everyone else!" He was plainly exas-perated with Germaine on this occasion. "There they were, everyone else was keeping quiet, Schlegel was giving himself one compliment after another for his disdain for high society, and there she was, telling every-one how gifted she was at the art of conversation. For the rest of us the only entertainment we could derive was to compare the eulogies that each was reciting at the expense of the other."

But Benjamin was honest; he knew that he could never escape and he said so in his diary. "Ten years ago," he wrote, "I saw Biondetta [this was one of his names for Germaine; another was Minette] for the first time, and she made my life for me. Since that time not a single day has passed without her having an influence over me, and I must say there hasn't been a day when she hasn't given me more trouble than pleasure."

There were days, of course, when he dreamed of freedom. On the 28th of November, 1804, he wrote: "I must write a letter to Biondetta. I shall suggest either marriage or a breakup, and I shall add to my letter that a final understanding must be reached by an exact date. My letter will be charming, reasonable, sweet but firm, and I'll tell her I'm setting out on a journey lasting four years, and I won't come back un-less she agrees to marry me."

On the 4th of December he was willing to be miser-able. "What my life lacks is a plan," he wrote. "With-out Minette, I'd have a plan. But with her, there are difficulties."

Forty-eight hours later he was happy once again to be her prisoner. "A lovely day with Minette," he noted. "No one knows how to appreciate this woman better than I. She and I are forever thinking along the same lines. It is true that there is often a discrepancy between what she says and what she feels and how she acts. Led at the very beginning by the indulgence of her father, and later by the flattery of people around her, to seek her distractions and amusements in the great world, she was so successful and so brilliant when she first began to play a role in society that she has never given up the dreadful habit of basing her happiness on that of the people around her, and of counting on their backing as though it were her due. But this fault of hers, which is the source of all her unhappiness and mine, is less evident every day, while her affection for me is constantly increasing. There is certainly a good deal of truth in what she said about the embarrassment our marriage would create for the life she leads and for the careers of her children. If I were egotistical, I shouldn't mind; but being the sort of person I am, I'd never forgive myself if I did her real harm, or even imaginary harm. The idea of a secret marriage may be the best way out. Whatever happens, whether the marriage be secret or public, it must take place this winter."

And then, on the very next day, Benjamin was racked with doubts. "I had a talk this evening with Minette," he told his diary. "It's always the same story. She has to be unhappy, her feelings are easily hurt, she's immensely clever, and she's even kinder than she is clever. She has a real need for me, which makes her very attractive, but makes me very miserable. To leave her would be the same thing as sacrificing her completely to my convenience, and that would be as cruel as condemning her to a horrible punishment for the sake of some gain to me."

Came the 11th of December and Benjamin and Germaine parted. He was setting out for Les Herbages, his home at Maffliers near Paris, and she, accompanied by August Wilhelm von Schlegel and her three children, was on her way to Italy. They parted knowing that they would be forever inseparable, knowing that no diversion, no matter how entertaining or how reassuring for the moment, could claim either for long. "It was very hard on her," Benjamin recorded in his diary. "It's strange, my feeling for her. I am much happier without her, but the thought that she might be unhappy would make me give up my life to consoling her. Now I'll have five or six months when I shall be on my own."

In Milan Germaine found a certain compensation for Benjamin's absence in the company of the poet Vincenzo Monti, but the comparison was fatal to the Italian even though little Albertine declared that her mother loved only two things about Italy, the sea and Monti.

"It is impossible," Germaine said on introducing herself to Monti on December 30, "for anyone who is interested in literature to have pronounced your name without admiration, or have missed reading your poetry, which upholds the honor of modern literature in Italy. It's for that reason that I asked for a letter of introduction to you." She said she would be at home all day until seven in the evening, and she did not wait in vain.

Before January was over, she was telling this new admirer that she *had* to write him letters, but her correspondence (at least all that has been published) could not have given Benjamin an anxious moment. "How can I," she asked, "have fallen in just two weeks into the habit of writing you? But I have. All I've done was to recognize who you were. I felt there was something of myself in you, you were like a friend waiting for me, certainly you weren't a new acquaintance. My rights over you can't possibly date from yesterday; for years we have been thinking the same thoughts."

Monti was a comfortable poet; his efforts are recalled

only by the compilers of the larger reference works. He was overjoyed when Germaine wrote him: *You must realize that you have found a sister.* "A sister!" he answered. "I believe I am worthy to hear that sacred word."

Monti could not possibly comprehend Germaine's revulsion at the sight of the apparently eternal inertia of the peninsula. On her way to Rome she stopped at Parma to call on Bodoni, found that he had wit enough to ply his trade as a printer, but sensed that he had next to no ambition. "If he were really an intellectual," she told Monti, "what a dreary life he'd be leading in this city." She was more than dismayed by the swarms of beggars and indolent priests she encountered in the streets of Parma; she was disgusted. Germaine's impatience would have been completely shared by Giacomo Leopardi; the creator of *I Canti* was, however, not yet seven years old when she made her entrance into the Holy City.

In Rome itself Germaine may have read over more than once a letter she had received from Joseph Bonaparte before leaving Coppet. "When you visit the Coliseum and the other monuments whose inscriptions you can barely make out, remember that there is one man in France who is interested in your return. Take all the pleasure you can in the marvels of the ancient and modern worlds, and have no fear that you are wasting time that could be better spent in begging to come back here. I'll take care of that, I promise you, but I must ask you to resign yourself courageously to whatever happens, and to have confidence in my friendship. If I don't succeed, no one can."

She was, she confessed, somewhat disappointed by her first impressions of Rome. "So far," she wrote Monti on the 5th of February, "I've only seen Saint Peter's and a few cardinals who've come to see me and are all ready to turn me into a Catholic. . . . The most beautiful monuments have been erected in honor of the greatest superstitions, and the second one begins to remember the greatness of the past, one is faced with the blackest misery on all sides. . . . People here are constantly recalling the heights from which man has fallen: what man is, and what he was, is a subject fit to inspire a fit of melancholy that's more humiliating than delightful."

Two days later she was only partly reconciled. "I must talk to you about Rome," she confided to Monti once again. "It's all very beautiful, very majestic, very melancholy. I love Rome on a moonlit night, when we are nearer the ancient world and the ruins come to life. But Roman society! Roman men! Ah, Monti, what I most admire about you is that you have remained yourself in spite of all this!"

To which the ever-patient Monti made a patient reply. "The moral standards of Rome could not possibly be of any interest to you, but think of the Roman genius for the fine arts, the monuments to the grandeur of the ancient world, the precious legacy of the centuries, and the majestic but sweet melancholy that comes over the soul when one contemplates the past, living with the great men who are no longer here! A soul like yours should not try to find any diversion in the society of the princes of Holy Church, but should wander among the ruins of the Forum and inspect the great art collections."

Monti's advice was sincere but austere. Germaine found amusements of her own. She had been charmed by what she heard of the Academy of the Arcadia, an organization founded in the late seventeeth century, whose members—so they claimed—modeled their verse on that of the ancient shepherds of Arcadia in the Golden Age. When Abbate Luigi Godard of the Arcadians invited her to attend a meeting of the society and to favor them with the sound of her voice, she agreed to recite a French translation of her own of one of Monti's sonnets, whereupon Prince Chigi read a pretty poem in Germaine's honor, and Abbate Godard pronounced her an Arcadian. "Sonnets fell like warm rain upon us," she wrote Monti. "Ten young men, each one declaiming with mounting fury, attacked us with sonnets that rang like so many thunderbolts from the Vatican. Think of all that energy wasted!"

In the meantime Benjamin arrived at what he believed was a decision. "My plans have now been made," he put down in his diary for the 7th of February. "I'll let Minette stay on in Milan. Then I'll write her proposing a secret marriage, and I'll tell her I insist on it. The more I love her, the harder it is for me to leave her or cause her any inconvenience, which means that I must take a definite stand."

Twenty-four hours later—he had not yet written the letter—he was again thinking of asking Germaine to be his wife. "Two months from now," he reflected, "I'll write Minette and tell her that since I'm giving up my country for her, my library, and the opportunity to do any work, not to mention the chance to make a connection with other rich women, the only fair thing for her to do is to marry me. I'll wait for her answer, and if she says no, I'll go and live in Berlin or Weimar. And now let's get down to work."

Benjamin was not delighted by Germaine's account of her reception by the Arcadians. "She is simply enchanted with her success in Rome," he noted. "A lot of good that will do her." He was positive—and he was not wrong—that Monti's sonnet was a sentimental rendering of a religious theme, quite unworthy of being translated into acceptable French. "She has really behaved like a clown," he went on. "If that sonnet ever crosses the French border, she really will be ridiculous. They'll think she has tried to win a new reputation for her piety. With all her intelligence, and with all the kindness she is capable of, how sad it is to see that she makes so much of trifles."

March came, and Germaine began playing the game that Benjamin had invented in his evenings at Les Herbages. "I have been studying," he recorded on the 12th, "the notion of a secret marriage that Minette has brought up. Everything considered, I think I must accept her offer and hold her to it in the event she wishes to retreat. It is evident that we shall never break up. Once that point is made clear, I must insist on the most firm and legal attachment."

There were difficulties, as he understood. "She kept trying to get her father out of Coppet, where he wanted to live. She'll drive me into living at Coppet, where I have no desire to be. If I'm not an imbecile, I'll stand my ground, and we'll each go our own ways. But what if I am an imbecile?"

By the 1st of April Benjamin was again—so he thought—on the eve of making a decision. "I won't live in Coppet or anywhere in Switzerland, unless our marriage is in the open." Then, on the 13th, came another letter from Germaine. "It will be very difficult for me to leave her. Every day she is growing more affectionate and more charming. I must arrange my life with her as best I can. But not in Switzerland, not in Geneva, please."

In the interval Germaine had gone down to Naples, and again she told Monti her misgivings concerning Italian society. "Everything is delightful here," she wrote, "with the exception of the moral climate which reminds me that I am not in paradise."

It was inevitable that the one attachment Germaine made in Italy was not an Italian, even though he happened to be born in Turin. Dom Pedro de Souza, Duca de Palmella, with whom she consoled herself as she could not with Monti, was a young Portuguese of twenty-four whose father's diplomatic career had taken him to Copenhagen, Berlin, and Rome. On Germaine's return from Naples to the Holy City, she strolled with Dom Pedro in the moonlight of the Coliseum, and for once Benjamin might have been uneasy.

"The wreck of time," she wrote Dom Pedro after their walk among the ruins, "has reminded us that we belong to the present. We are as one in our devotion to what is beautiful on earth, and my father in paradise must have forgiven my happiness, mixed as it was with tears and vexed by problems." She went on to promise that Dom Pedro would shortly appear in a novel she was already constructing. "I have written down some of the things you said that night. I couldn't invent anything to compare with your conversation, and I look forward to the secret understanding there will be between us when you read *Corinne*."

Early in May she was still in Rome, still close to Dom Pedro. "Keep this poetry of mine," she wrote him, "until you are alone in a place where not a word I have said can be repeated, or until the time comes when nothing matters to a woman, say, when you return to Portugal, or ten years from now. If you came back this evening at eleven, we could walk over to see the Coliseum by moonlight."

The poem she forwarded was uninspired, but Germaine was unquestionably fond of Dom Pedro. "If you are the man I think you are," she wrote him a little later from Florence, "you'll love me for a time, but not forever, for fate has made too great a difference in our ages, but you will have your troubles when you come to give someone else my place in your heart, and the choice you make will prove that I made no mistake in thinking so much of you." She began to wonder whether Dom Pedro might prove to be the perfect husband for Albertine. However, Albertine was only nine years old at the time.

Germaine made still another appeal to Dom Pedro from Florence. "Of all the compliments I've received here," she told him, "there is only one that I can never forget. A Russian told me that when he came into the gallery at Florence, the sound of my voice was more attractive than that of any other woman there. Dear Dom Pedro, you've heard that voice of mine tell you again and again how much I love you. Listen to it once more, when you are all alone, in the places where I wish I were."

In June she was back at Coppet; in July Benjamin joined her. On the 19th he set down in his diary "2.2.7.7.7." and also "3.3.2.3.2.2." He intended the code to be translated; two months before this, he decided that the numeral 2 was to represent his desire to break the tie that bound him, 7, plans for traveling, and 3, the fact that he was once more a prisoner, entangled by her fleeting charms.

Benjamin stayed on and on, to the concern of August Wilhelm von Schlegel, who had appreciated his absence on the Italian journey. There came a time when August Wilhelm could no longer contain himself. "I am helpless," he wrote Germaine. "I need to be loved. . . . You were unhappy," he recalled, thinking of Necker's death, "and I made up my mind in a second to stand by you. But then, in no time at all, I too became unhappy. When you began to draw near me, you were happy, although far away from the first object of your affections. Everything seemed simple to you, and you were far from demanding. How you have changed since! First of all, an old attachment has assumed all of its former claims, and you never once told me it meant that much to you. . . . I am the last on the scene, and I fear I shall always be nothing but that."

Germaine could not refuse to listen to August Wilhelm's prayers. On the 18th of October, 1805, she soothed his feelings at Coppet by allowing him to present her with a signed agreement. It read as follows:

"You have asked for a promise in writing, my lovely friend; you thought I hesitated to make such a promise. Here it is.

"I declare that you have every claim upon me, and that I have none upon you. You may dispose of my person and my life as you see fit. You may give orders. You may forbid me to do certain things. I shall obey you in every respect. I do not look for any happiness in this world except for that which you may bestow upon me."

Whether Benjamin was aware of the existence of this agreement—so similar to the pledges he and Germaine signed at the beginning of their relationship—is a question. Judging from his diary, the fall of 1805 was not altogether idyllic. One entry, made a month before the pact with Schlegel, may be significant. "A great discovery: she could be happy without me. So I'm doing myself a favor by staying at her side."

Of course Benjamin understood that happiness was a state of mind that Germaine never could condone. Her ambitions could not possibly be satisfied. This was something which Chateaubriand found hard to comprehend; in September he sought to comfort her by reminding her that "one has to live one's own life all by one's self. Anyone should be happy who, like a bee, has a honeycomb and a little honey on hand with which to pass the winter. As for myself, I'm only a miserable gnat, without even a hole in a tree to hide in."

To Germaine this was comfortable advice, and because it was comfortable, worthless. She had not given up hope of regaining Paris, even though the Emperor had made himself more than plain on that subject. "Let her friends know," he wrote Fouché, the master of his spy system, "that she must come no nearer than forty leagues. All subversive elements must be driven out of Paris. When I am 2,000 leagues away, at the other end of Europe, I can't possibly allow disloyal subjects to have a free hand in stirring up trouble in my capital."

With this edict still in force, the mistress of Coppet was driven to seek what consolations she could in her father's house. One consolation was the establishment of a private theater. Voltaire had set a certain standard not too long ago at his home at Ferney; Germaine was anxious to do even better. She and her friends staged Voltaire's *Mérope* by the end of December; in February they essayed his *Mahomet*. And then, after presenting *Agar*, a slender piece written by Germaine herself, in which little Albertine was featured, they came to the conclusion of the season with *Phèdre*.

August Wilhelm von Schlegel, who approved of all these efforts, was particularly pleased by Germaine's performance in the title role of Racine's masterpiece. "You may imagine our expectations," he wrote, "which were based upon the development of the part up until this time. But Madame de Staël surprised us. She amazed us. Her acting was really in the grand style."

This was not all that August Wilhelm had to say on the subject. "She has the gift," he explained in an essay devoted to Germaine's new talent, "of arousing the best in everyone according to his own abilities, and so had everyone excited. In no time at all she gathered around her a group of talented and devoted people who were willing to obey her every command, and to bring out the essence of the plays in question. Even the outward appearance of things left little to be desired, thanks to the taste she showed in selecting and observing the costumes. The result was that the smallness of our stage was no disadvantage whatever. . . .

"If I could only describe," he went on, "how her desire for inner truth led her to overcome all formal limitations, how she breathed new life into the regular beat of the lines, warming them with the fullness of her heart, lifting them through her enthusiasm to the noblest form of poetry."

Having paid so many compliments in print to his hostess, he felt free, in a letter to one of his sisters-in-law, to speak of his own success in *Mérope*. "I have had something to say about the costumes," he wrote, "and although I have to recite French verses, I like to think that my tunic and my gestures will mark me as a Greek."

August Wilhelm may have made a noble entrance on the stage of Coppet, but he could not hope to rival the impression created during this theatrical season by Prosper de Barante. Prosper was only twenty-three when he began to call on Germaine.

Prosper's father, Claude-Ignace de Barante, was an amiable man, far from the ideal spy on life at Coppet, although keeping close watch on the château was one of his duties as Napoleon's representative at Geneva. Since 1798 the city had been under French occupation. "She is high-minded," the austere Barante told his son, "and she has an intellect far above that of anyone else. But she is indiscreet, she is a far from happy woman, she is disgusted with what's going on, and she has no hope for the future."

Claude-Ignace had his misgivings; Prosper had none. By the fall of 1804 he was writing Germaine from Paris that the French people were sick of the tyranny of Napoleon. By the spring of 1805 he was urging her to buy a house as near Paris as possible. "In the country," he pointed out, "you might enjoy even more free-

F

dom than in the center of espionage."

Although Benjamin was in and out of Coppet in the fall and winter of 1805 and 1806, Prosper and Germaine came ever closer to reaching an understanding. In September Prosper conceived that she might one day be his wife. "Good-by," he wrote her after one of his visits to the château. "I love you and I am happy. Sometimes, when I am holding you in my arms, I am sorry that I can't be entirely yours. But when I listen to my heart, I know that nothing can be deeper than my feeling for you, and that I need no outward sign to declare myself yours forever."

When April came, and Germaine, surrendering to her desire to see France once more, set out with Schlegel and her children for Auxerre in Burgundy, Prosper followed. His father was disappointed. "There is a melancholy, misanthropic tone to your last letter," Claude-Ignace wrote, "which can only be explained by the situation in which you find yourself. I avoided Madame de Staël all winter, and I see now that I didn't keep far enough away from her. In your place I shouldn't have gone to Auxerre. I should have spent all my strength to keep away from the struggle."

But Prosper could not be so cautious. After one of his trips to Vincelles near Auxerre, where Germaine had rented the villa of a Swiss banker, he implored his father to write to Germaine. To Claude-Ignace this was absurd. "I am," he wrote, "sending back to you the draft of the letter you asked me to lose no time in sending to Auxerre. I can't imagine anything more insane. There is no word, not a single word in your letter to relieve the impression I have of the horrible position in which that woman has placed you. She is robbing you of all your common sense, all your judgment, all your kindness, and all your gratitude. Do you intend to go on wasting your time and wrecking your health making one trip after another, losing your sleep and your money, all for a woman who, as you've told me and other people, has no sense of duty, for a woman who is poisoning my life and ruining yours? You must be the victim of some supernatural power which makes you act against your own will, which makes you say in all seriousness the silly things you've been saying about this trip. Perhaps I should not be surprised by the cold and distant language you use in speaking to your father! Anything is believable, anything is possible, thanks to the madness to which that woman has led you. Exactly what is going on between you? You give me your word of honor that you're not in love and not thinking of marriage. What do all those words mean if the feeling you have for her is more demanding than love itself? I pity you from the bottom of my heart for not having the character to break the ties that bind you."

This was not a tranquil summer. Prosper was not the only devoted friend who made the trip to Vincelles. Dom Pedro passed by on his way to Spain. Benjamin made his inevitable appearance. And then, as June turned into July, Juliette talked of coming. "If you are serious about that delightful idea," Germaine wrote her, "come with Mathieu *and not with Prosper*, who might take all the time I'd like to give to you alone."

It was evident that Prosper de Barante had made more than an impression. In the end Juliette was detained.

In September, when Germaine pushed on toward Rouen, she was troubled by the suspicion that Prosper and Juliette in Paris might be more than friends. "How soon will you come to see me, now that we are so near?" she asked Juliette. "When will you let me enjoy the pleasures that I enjoy more than anyone else? You say that you'll be writing me more often now that you're seeing more of Prosper. I fear, I must tell you, that you'll let him fall in love with you, and that would be a great sorrow for me, for two of the ties I hold dear would be threatened. Don't allow him to do that, Juliette. You know that I am banished, you know that I trust you, you know that I can never be as attractive as you are. You will be too generous to indulge in the slightest flirtation. It's not that I really believe in his affection for me. I'm so unhappy, I doubt he is really in love with me. But the thought my unhappiness might be due to you is more than I could bear. I wouldn't have the strength to stand it. (Let this be between us.)"

This was an anxious letter, written, Germaine soon learned, in what was a desperate time for Juliette. Her husband had gone into bankruptcy. "Ah, my dear Juliette," she wrote on the 17th of November, "how sad it was for me to hear the horrible news! How I curse my exile, which makes it impossible for me to be at your side, and to press you against my heart.

"You have," Germaine went on, "lost everything which makes life charming, but if it were possible for you to be loved more dearly, and to be closer to me, that is exactly what would happen." She reminded her friend that she was still the greatest beauty in Europe, that her character was stainless, that she was and would be a proud and generous woman, in spite of her husband's ruin. "Dear Juliette, don't forget that we are the ones who enjoyed all the luxury that surrounded you. Your good fortune was ours. And I feel that I am bankrupt because you are no longer wealthy."

In the meantime Germaine was beginning to understand that Claude-Ignace de Barante would have none of her. "I don't know what will become of me," she wrote Prosper's father. "France has no meaning for me without him. Why do you heap reproaches upon me, if I am never to see him again? He loves you so much, and I love you, too, although you have done me so much harm. Please help me as much as you can, and pity me if I can put up no resistance."

Worst of all, Prosper was growing cautious. "Of course," he jotted down in his diary, "to be loved by her is a unique experience, but nevertheless, love has its own rules which must be taken into consideration, unless one wishes to feel unhappy and guilty. And she believes that there is nothing better than hurling oneself upon the flames; she has a real respect for people who have gone mad or turned criminal for such an end."

"I ask you," Germaine pleaded with Claude-Ignace, "not to rob me of the wreck of your son's affection for me. Don't let me turn into a bitter woman; I'd much rather think the best of both of you in spite of all the harm you have done me." No answer came from Geneva.

In her despair Germaine drew nearer to Paris. In January, 1807, she received official permission to settle at the Château d'Acosta near Aubergenville, only twelve leagues from the city. Tempted beyond endurance, she raced on to Paris itself for a few days. Not daring to appear by daylight, she took long walks on moonlit nights, and once she presumed to call upon Madame de Tessé, an old lady whom Thomas Jefferson had found charming and whom Necker had known very well indeed. Madame de Tessé had once declared that "if I were a queen, I'd order Madame de Staël to talk to me forever." But the old lady was horrified by Germaine's indiscretion. Fouché was informed, and when the mistress of the Château d'Acosta bought the Château de Cernay at Franconville, only *four* leagues away from Paris, the lightning struck.

It was obvious that the official who granted her the right to move to Aubergenville was out of touch with the Emperor. On the last day of 1806, from Putulsk in Poland, Napoleon made himself quite clear. "Don't let that wretch Madame de Staël come near Paris," he ordered.

The Emperor was hardly up to date on the situation when he wrote Fouché on April 18. "I am," he announced, "happy to say that nothing more has been heard of Madame de Staël. When I do take action, *I'll have the facts to go on.* That woman is an old crow. She thought that we were in terrible trouble, and was concocting all kinds of mad plots. Let her go and live by Lake Leman. Haven't those Genevans done us enough damage already?"

On the 7th of May Napoleon was in possession of all the facts. The battle of Friedland was in the offing, but a reprimand was due, and a reprimand was issued. "I see by your bulletin of April 27th," he told Fouché, "that Madame de Staël left for Geneva on the 21st. I am sorry that you are so badly informed. Madame de Staël was in Paris on the 24th, 25th, 26th, 27th, and 28th, and is probably still in Paris. She has gone to a number of dinner parties with literary people.

"If Madame de Staël's head had not been stuffed with nonsense, we should not be in this mess, and she would have calmed down. By not making it plain that she had no hope of coming back to Paris and starting her campaign of lies all over again, we have made life more miserable than ever for that woman, and got her in real trouble, *for I'll see to it that the police take care of the problem.*"

The Emperor was made even angrier by an appeal he had just received from Germaine herself. "That insane Madame de Staël," he wrote Fouché, "has just written me a six-page letter, gibberish all of it, in which I discovered no end of pomposity and almost no common sense. She tells me she has bought some land in the valley of Montmorency. She goes on from there to conclude that she may live in Paris. I must tell you once again, if we give her any such hope we are tormenting her unjustly. *If I gave you the complete story of what she has been up to in her country house for the two months she has been there, you would be astonished, for although I am 500 leagues away from Paris, I know more about what's going on there than the head of my police force.*"

Germaine at last understood that to breathe the air of Paris was to invite disaster. Yet she clung for a moment or two to the half-shattered hope that a work of art might melt Napoleon's heart. In April she had published her new novel, *Corinne*. Stopping at Lyon for the night of May 7th on her flight to Coppet, she dropped a line to Juliette. "You have *Corinne* now," she wrote her friend. "Let me hear what they are saying about it in the literary world, and if you hear no bad news about it from the government, for I'm expecting some relief from the sad situation I'm in. It seems to me that if anything can disarm my enemies, so innocent an occupation may turn the trick."

She went on to Coppet, and it was well that she did, for the Emperor was not pleased. "I cannot forgive Madame de Staël for running down the French," he commented, which was his way of acknowledging in the cast of the novel the presence of the Comte d'Erfeuil, a most precise Frenchman who would have no slurs cast on the classics of French literature. If the conqueror of Friedland had been a connoisseur of architecture, he might have been more lenient, might even have forgiven his opponent for writing this book. Her wandering in Italy was admittedly aimless, her affection for Monti, even her romances with Dom Pedro de Souza and Prosper de Barante were more a matter for sighs than for sobs, yet this was the stuff out of which she contrived a two-volume work which raised an unmistakable façade around her existence since her father's death.

The Corinne of the title page was not just another luckless woman; she was Germaine on a heroic scale. "Her arms were strikingly beautiful. She had a good but emphatic figure, like that of a Greek statue, a symbol of youth and happiness." This self-portrait would have been absurd if Germaine had failed to reveal that her heroine was generous; it was the very violence of Corinne's generosity that made the implausible plausible and the novel a success.

Oswald, Lord Nelvil, the Scottish peer who plays the hero's role, is, like Dom Pedro de Souza and Prosper de Barante, a disappointing lover. He is charmed by Corinne, whom he meets on the day she is crowned on the Capitoline Hill for her achievements as a poetess, but he is eventually induced by his father's injunction to desert her and to marry her half-sister Lucile. At the very end, at Corinne's deathbed, his reason is despaired of, but there are grounds for believing that he may go on living much in the manner of Souza or Barante.

There are moments when Oswald is as solemn as Germaine herself when face to face with Italian civilization. "In this nation," the highborn Scot tells Corinne, "where love is the only thing they think of, there is not a single novel. The reason for that is that love is so instantaneous, so public, that no stage of development is ever reached, and if she had to tell the true story of what goes on, the beginning and the ending would be on the very first page."

As a libretto, *Corinne* would have suited Donizetti better than Verdi, for it is more rapturous than reflective. Listen, for example, to Corinne's words at the sight of the Coliseum. "These admirable ruins," she says, "convey the impression of so much magnificence and genius that one can easily be tempted to make a mistake and attribute real grandeur to them, bestowing on a work of art the admiration which is only proper for the monuments of a generous civilization."

As one might expect of a young woman who responds in such a fashion to the Coliseum, Corinne, when the time comes, agrees to give harp lessons in Florence to Juliette, the child of Oswald and Lucile. Her father trembles on hearing her pluck a Scottish air from the instrument. "Was it," he asks, "the lady on the bank of the Arno who taught you to play like that?" "Yes," little Juliette answers, "but it was terribly difficult for her. More than once she was too upset to go on. I begged her several times to stop, but she wouldn't hear of it. The only thing she wanted was for me to promise to play this tune every year on a certain day, the 17th of November, I believe. . . ."

A little while, and Corinne takes it upon herself to call on her half-sister Lucile. "Since," she tells her, "I must die very shortly, I must tell you that I have only one wish, and that is for Oswald to find in you and his daughter some traces of my stay on earth, and that Oswald may never enjoy a second of happiness without recalling Corinne."

This, of course, was exactly the impression that Germaine desired to leave with Dom Pedro de Souza and Prosper de Barante. Aiming for an audience, she reached it; there were thousands of women in the early nineteenth century who fancied themselves in Corinne's position.

But *Corinne*, in the final analysis, was a public performance. And this could be no more than a momentary distraction for Germaine. She knew, as she hurried on to Coppet, that she prized the devotion of only one man. The crisis in her attachment to Benjamin could not be postponed forever.

CHAPTER ELEVEN

BENJAMIN THE
INCURABLE

Perhaps the most disappointed reader of *Corinne* was Prosper de Barante. "You've been cruelly reproaching me," he wrote Germaine early in the summer of 1807, "and now you have shut me up in that Oswald, and I have no way of defending myself." If, Prosper reflected, Oswald "could write down an account of what he had been through, then anyone could tell how deeply he suffered. I'm not sure he was meant to be a happy man, but I do know that his chance for happiness is gone forever. He is in a false position, and all his youth has been wasted, just because he met Corinne."

Prosper was saddened by the use to which Germaine put his affection; no one likes to be taken for an unheroic hero. He was also infuriated when he came to realize that he could not count in her world. He was not—this was now clear to him—sufficiently exasperating to be more than a passing fancy. There was a passage in the novel that told him more than he had ever guessed about the author. "I wouldn't think of opening my window to see the Bay of Naples for the first time," Corinne confessed, "but I'd travel 500 leagues for a good talk with a man I didn't know."

Benjamin Constant was now back at Coppet, and Prosper could contemplate the extremes to which Germaine would run for a man whom no one could hope to know.

Benjamin himself was inclined to question the opportunities at his disposal. "I have seen her again," he wrote his cousin Rosalie on the 20th of July, "and no matter what anyone believes about the distractions she was enjoying while she was writing me those horrible letters, I have had a thousand and one proofs of her grief, which was horrifying. The moment I arrived, it was ghastly. She is such a combination of violence and affection that I am shaken from head to foot, and I know that I can't go on living with the perpetual anguish with which I am afflicted by her reproaches, her complaints, her outbursts, and her states of depression. Nor can I stand the thought of destroying a tie which she is determined to hold on to at any cost. I have tried to reason with her, but all to no avail."

On the 5th of August Benjamin was even more miserable. "I have had all I can stand of this uncertain way of life," he reported in his diary. "It has turned me into a worn-out tramp, made me frightfully unhappy, kept me from using my head, eaten up all of my money, and been very bad for my character."

There were, as he saw it, five alternatives open to him. He could break, once and for all, with Madame de Staël. He could give her the choice of marrying him or seeing the last of him. He could enjoy life as an independent bachelor. He could settle down in Switzerland with a proper wife. Or, and this notion was beginning to be tempting, he could take up where he had left off with Charlotte von Hardenberg, the good and trusting woman with whom he had been so close at the court of Brunswick fourteen years before.

Benjamin's logic was as relentless as usual, his kindness was indisputable, and if he failed to use common sense, this was not surprising. Reason had often led him down unreasonable avenues.

Still married to the Baron von Marenholz when Benjamin set off for Switzerland and his first meeting with Germaine, Charlotte had divorced the Baron to become, in 1798, the wife of the Vicomte du Tertre, a French émigré who now and then pretended to be a devout Roman Catholic. She had followed her husband to Paris in 1802, and there one evening she heard Benjamin's name mentioned in the course of a dinner party. He was, someone said, having financial difficulties. This was all the encouragement she needed to resume her correspondence with her former lover. She wrote him more than once; early in 1805 she was pleased to receive a note asking if he might come to call. He eventually did, although he set down in his diary that he was, on one occasion, far too lazy to make the effort.

He called again and again on Charlotte, possibly because he felt a certain obligation to a woman for whom he had once held something resembling affection. "That woman," he declared in his diary for the 11th of January, 1805, "is very sorry to see how little love I have left for her. What can I do about it? I talk my head off to be entertaining, but all that I feel for her is a sincere friendship. Her husband is beginning to be jealous. However, he has no need to worry. I don't turn up too often."

Charlotte was in earnest, as Benjamin discovered before January was over. On the 26th he noted that he had spent a long, sad, and occasionally boring evening in her company. "If I don't watch out, I'll upset her life once again. I had that feeling tonight when I was with her. Where will all this lead? Looking at things from another standpoint, I might find it rather monotonous if I sympathized with her over her absurd marriage without doing anything to improve her lot or brighten her future. I shall have to call less frequently."

When Benjamin came by four days later, he found her in tears. "I don't know what she may have put into her husband's head. She merely told me a word or two which made it plain that I was involved. I'll have to get away from all this."

Although the history of religions was one of Benjamin's major concerns at this period, and he did a certain amount of meditating on the religious practices of the Egyptians, he found that he could not resist opening Charlotte's letters. Late in February he found that her latest communication was better than he had expected. "She may have some justification for her conduct," he declared in his diary. "I shall see her, but it won't do her any good; nothing can be more tiresome than this sort of thing when one is not in love with a woman."

By the 5th of March Benjamin was no longer quite so certain of himself. "This woman really isn't very interesting," he noted, "but she has a great many good qualities. I'll see her tomorrow." When he came the next day he found that he was not in the least in love with her, but he had to admit he was moved by her deep affection for him. "If she weren't already married," he decided on the 10th, "I might marry her and find some peace of mind. . . . But let's stop thinking of the impossible." It was only on the 21st that he proposed to put an end to their meetings. "I can't see her any more at her house," he discovered, "even if she insisted on my coming, and I certainly won't allow her to see me elsewhere."

On the 26th Benjamin was positive that the end had come. Charlotte had written him that her husband was threatening him with a duel; this was too silly. "If something else were involved, I'd take on my opponent," he reflected. "But I can't be accused of rushing a woman into a divorce when I'm not in the least interested in such a thing, and besides, if she were divorced, I shouldn't marry her."

Came April, however, and he was relenting. "I'll see her tomorrow at my house. I may have a hard time, but I can't help doing my best to console someone so lovely and so charming."

And on the 4th of May he was, he imagined, ready for anything. "I've made up my mind," he told himself. "If she can regain her freedom, I'll marry her." He had just received a disappointing letter from Germaine, and was rather pleased to hear that Charlotte's husband was agreeable to the thought of a German divorce.

Yet in June, 1805, he was back at Coppet. "You are," Charlotte wrote him, "going to see that woman again who has done me so much harm without knowing it. I must be incapable of hatred, for I don't hate her."

So Benjamin drifted until, in the fall of 1806, he got a letter from Germaine that made him suddenly anxious for the security that Charlotte seemed to offer. "I can't stand this slavery any longer," he jotted down in his notebook, "and with every day that passes I sense that it has become more necessary and less troublesome to break this tie."

On the 26th of October he wrote a letter to Charlotte that might have been final if signed by anyone other than Benjamin Constant. "I must have her," he put down in his diary. "It's all too insane. This woman, whom I've said no to a hundred times, who has kept offering herself day after day, whom I've always shunted aside, whom I left eighteen months ago without an ounce of regret, and to whom I've written at least a hundred trifling letters—I took them all back last

Monday—this is the woman who has succeeded in making me lose my head. For me not to see her is a terrible punishment. Perhaps Madame de Staël is largely responsible for all this. The contrast between her petulance, her egotism, and her constant watching out for herself, and the sweetness and calm, the really modest behavior of Charlotte makes Charlotte a thousand times more dear to me.

"I am," he concluded, "sick and tired of the man-woman who has kept me in chains for ten years now—a woman who is really a woman is intoxicating and enchanting."

It was about this time that he made the mistake of telling Germaine that he had been seeing something of Charlotte. "Good heavens! You've been talking!" was Charlotte's comment in a letter to Benjamin. "I am horribly upset. Don't allow her to sacrifice the happiness of someone who has not intended to do her any harm. Far from it! People say she is good and noble and generous. For someone like that, there is no consolation in causing someone else to be unhappy. Tell her that I shall love her, too, and that instead of losing one friend she'll win a second. She is so sensitive that she'll know how to appreciate warm affection. Let her dispose of me, too. Anything that will make you a happier man will be a source of kindness to me."

He was, of course, back at Coppet for the summer of 1807. This was the summer that Chateaubriand recalled as one party after another. "The world was unsettled." he admitted. "But it sometimes happens that the echo of great catastrophes doubles the enchantment of the joy of being young; we are never more likely to abandon ourselves to a life of pleasure than when we fear that pleasure is about to be lost forever."

Coppet was crowded. Monti ran up from Milan. Schlegel, as usual, was on hand. Prosper de Barante returned for another glance at the woman who had driven him to desperation. And John Izard Middleton of Middleton Place, South Carolina, a young man of twenty-two who had not yet published his careful drawings of Grecian remains in Italy, came to gaze at Juliette Récamier.

When the theater at Coppet reopened, Juliette consented to play the part of the angel in her hostess's drama of *Agar dans le Désert*. In *Phèdre*, although Germaine assumed the title role, it was Juliette as Aricie who caused the greater sensation. According to one in the audience that night, a shudder ran over all the spectators the second Juliette appeared.

She had, as all this world knew, fallen in love with Prince August of Prussia. He had been taken prisoner at Eylau, and now he stopped in Switzerland on his way to Italy; on that very evening, he had taken his seat in Germaine's theater. When Juliette called out from the stage:

Partez, prince, et suivez vos généreux desseins
J'accepte tous les dons que vous voulez me faire . . .

the applause was certain and generous.

On the next morning the prince signed a document in which he swore, on his honor and in his anxiety to keep intact the purity of his feelings for Juliette, to do everything within his power to marry her. He also promised that he would never have another woman in his life as long as he had the chance of being her husband. Juliette signed a similar document, but when she heard that her husband was reluctant to divorce her, she had the delicacy to surrender her chance of walking as a princess in the avenues of Potsdam.

Juliette could abandon a claim she had only half made; Germaine could never retreat. Even before the summer had fairly begun, Benjamin was worried by the intemperance of her language. "I've found some letters here," he complained from Paris to his cousin Rosalie, "of the sort one wouldn't write to a professional murderer, and she has written a great many others to mutual friends, full of horrible things concerning my character."

At Coppet Benjamin grew even more alarmed. "She keeps on arguing that she must have me at her side." he told his cousin, "and she has the idea—since I tried to get away from her after leaving her in Paris—that she can't lose sight of me. At the very first indication of my setting off, she threatens to kill herself. Her children, her servants, the whole world knows about her threats, and everyone thinks that I am a monster for not having put an end to her sufferings. But nothing except the promise to give up every chance of escape could possibly calm her nerves. And since, on the one hand, I feel that with her disposition and after so much excitement there is no possibility of our having a happy marriage, and on the other hand, I know that she would only enter into a marriage with extreme reluctance, and if I forced her to do so, I can't really, in good faith, give her the guarantee she asks for. And to add to all this, I am very fond of her and I'm terribly upset. . . . I spend my days quarreling with her, and my nights crying over her."

In the meantime Charlotte was pursuing the advantage she had lately won. "You know, my dearest angel," she wrote him early in August, "how deeply in love with you I am, and you can imagine the prayers I keep on making for the success of your move. But I can't help fearing that once again you are deceiving yourself. . . . She has followed you over to Lausanne. She is deaf, you admit, to any entreaty made in the name of pity, generosity, or reason. She would rather see you dead than have you enjoy any happiness or lead any life away from her, and still you go on believing that public opinion will bring her around. How can you hope that public opinion will restrain a woman who has spent all her life defying the world, and who will stop at nothing to gain her ends? . . . You feel more deeply about her than you've been willing to admit. If that wasn't the case, it would be impossible for you to go on having your perpetual illusions about her."

This letter seems never to have reached Benjamin, which was just as well, for on the 1st of September his relations with Germaine reached a crisis. She had sent her carriage to call for him at Lausanne, and when he walked through the gateway of Coppet, he made the mistake of believing that the time had come to carry out at least one of the plans of action he had been debating for so many years. He offered to make Germaine his wife.

As Benjamin ought to have understood, the daughter of Necker, who had been enjoying his anxiety—and her own—ever since 1794, took his proposal for an insult. In her rage she collected Schlegel and her children and brought them all before her lover. "There," she screamed, "is the man who forces me to choose between killing myself or compromising your very existence and all the money you stand to inherit."

When Benjamin swore that in that case he would never marry her, Germaine grew even more violent. She threw herself to the floor, pulled out her handkerchief, and made what appeared to be an attempt to strangle herself. For the rest of the day he did his best to console her; on the next morning, still haggard with the horror of his experience, he set off alone on horseback for Lausanne and La Chaumière, Rosalie's villa. He could count, he thought, on his cousin to protect him from the next assault.

But he could not escape. He had barely arrived at

La Chaumière, where Rosalie led him into a room and locked the door for safety's sake, when in rushed Germaine. Rosalie looked down the stairwell. There she was, writhing at the foot of the stairs, her hair in wild confusion, her bosom bared. "Where is he?" Germaine shrieked. "I must find him." She was told that he was not at home, but the lie was pointless. Benjamin immediately began knocking to be released.

"I had to let him out," Rosalie wrote in her account of the day. "She heard him, she ran to him, she threw herself in his arms; then she fell to the floor cursing him."

"What right do you have," Rosalie asked, "to make him so unhappy and to wreck his life?" Whereupon Rosalie was insulted with a fury that shook the house.

By now Benjamin's cousin was beyond being surprised. "The result of all this was that she took him back to Coppet for another six weeks," wrote Rosalie. "He has been writing us very friendly letters from over there, but they are calm letters, proving that he is in the power of someone who is stronger than he is, and that he is really touched by this last terrible proof of her love for him."

Benjamin's first letter to Rosalie from Coppet was that of a conquered man. "For the moment," he wrote, "let's talk of nothing but our mutual friendship and of how much we mean to each other. I shall never stop thinking of you as my sister, and even if this Tuesday has convinced me that I can't leave a person who has so much to recommend her, and who loves me so deeply, I shall never forget that, in everything you tried to do for me, you thought only of my happiness."

Benjamin was somewhat more succinct in writing to a friend whose confidence he and Germaine shared. "Once again," he said, "I have learned, thanks to a recent and most important occurrence, that the happiness of Madame de Staël means more to me than life itself." In the meantime he devoted his leisure at Coppet to completing the translation of Schiller's *Wallenstein*, which he had begun at Germaine's insistence.

By the 1st of October he admitted that Germaine was so charming that he could once again become her slave without giving a second's thought to her violent scenes in the past or a second's anxiety to the scenes she might throw in the future. "Of the two women who are in love with me," he reflected, "one has done me a great deal of harm by not marrying me, and the other will do me a great deal of harm by marrying me. However, I continue praying that Charlotte will keep on being in love with me, and that she may regain her freedom."

He promised to leave Germaine by the middle of October, and he told Charlotte that he had Germaine's permission. But of course he did not keep his word; it was not until the 13th of December that he joined Charlotte at Besançon; the two of them then set out for Paris.

Germaine was already on her way to Munich with Schlegel; she followed him to Vienna where he was to deliver a course of public lectures. In the capital she was entertained by the Prince de Ligne, who was seventy-three but amusing. "You are beginning to be too well known," the prince warned her. "No one is afraid of you any longer. You are surprising because you are no longer astonishing, and you are most astonishing when people recall that you once were gay, forthright, and simple-hearted—as though that were all there was to you."

Germaine was also pleased with the company of Maurice O'Donnell, an Irishman of twenty-eight who had become a captain in the Austrian Army. But Benjamin did not lose his importance. When she heard that he was thinking of moving to the United States, she was distressed. "If he listens to his heart beat," she told a mutual friend, "it will tell him that such a thing would bring me to my grave. I live to think only of Benjamin."

Was her lover the victim of his own benevolence? So Benjamin reasoned early in 1808 when writing his cousin Rosalie. "Perhaps," he confessed, "I've done as much harm in my life as an evil man, but the reason was that I was afraid of doing harm. This may not redound to my credit, and I won't try to say there was any excuse for my conduct, but it may explain the kindness with which I have been treated by those who know me."

He was about to put Germaine's kindness to the test. On the 5th of June, 1808, the Archbishop of Paris having declared that Du Tertre's marriage to a Protestant was invalid, Benjamin and Charlotte were made man and wife by the Protestant pastor of Besançon. The groom was daring, but the groom was also timid. He succeeded in swearing the bride to secrecy for two or three months, at the end of which time he imagined that he might be able to reason with the woman who had been so unreasonable—and so irresistible.

On the 12th of July Benjamin was at Coppet once more, having said good-by to Charlotte near Neuchâtel. To his aunt, the Comtesse de Nassau, he wrote that he was completely satisfied with what he called his wife. "I have," he said, "had the pleasure of enjoying the kindness, the thoughtfulness, and the affection of a woman who should make me happy forever. There is something so pure, so natural, and so sweet in everything she says or does, that if I'm with her for only three hours at a stretch, I feel more calm and much more like myself."

For her part Charlotte could not keep from worrying while Benjamin was in Germaine's custody. "My angel," his wife wrote him from Sécheron near Geneva, where she was stopping with her aunt, "let me at least catch a glimpse of you! If only we could take a little walk! We are about to set off from here. In two hours we shall be in Geneva, and we're going right by the place where you are staying. If only I could see you from afar, I'd experience a moment of happiness."

Whether Charlotte caught sight of her husband on this excursion is not known. But Benjamin was undeniably alarmed by her daring to approach Coppet. He went over to call on Charlotte at Sécheron, and let her know that he had advised Germaine of the presence of the German ladies. In the interval Charlotte's aunt Frau von Decken succeeded in getting an introduction of her own.

"*Tous les jours me sont bons pour les dames allemandes*," came the word from Coppet, and the day came when Frau von Decken arrived with her daughter and son-in-law, Charlotte having decided to keep her distance. All went well, Benjamin reported to one of his relatives at Lausanne. The aunt proved to be very talkative but she was very well received—so well received that when Jacques Dupuch, who maintained an elegant mansion on the rue des Granges in Geneva, asked Frau von Decken and her party to meet Germaine for dinner under his Venetian chandeliers, Charlotte accepted the invitation.

No hint has been given of Germaine's attitude on this occasion. But Charlotte, when her aunt commented on her evident interest in a man who saw her so seldom, broke down when the evening was over and confessed that she was Madame Benjamin Constant. Had she done wrong? She was almost ready to apologize in her next letter to her husband. The treacherous calm, if calm it can be called, lasted the rest of the season. Benjamin and Germaine paid several visits to the German ladies at Sécheron. There was even a boat trip on the lake, with Charlotte and Germaine face to face.

Who had conquered was not decided even in December, when Germaine moved into Geneva for the winter and Benjamin at last made his way to Paris with Charlotte. For in Paris he put his wife up in town and went out to live by himself in the country; it was not every day that he appeared with her in public. Nor was the situation more carefully defined in the spring, when Benjamin and Charlotte traveled down to Sécheron.

It was on the afternoon of May 9, 1809, when Benjamin had gone off to Ferney, that the moment came, the moment that he had been delaying for almost a year. Charlotte sent a message to Coppet, begging Germaine's presence in Sécheron for an important communication.

"I have come," said Germaine at Charlotte's door, "because you are a Hardenberg." She stayed until four o'clock in the morning, undeterred by the fact that her rival, who was coming down with a cold, was plunging her feet in a mustard bath the second she made her appearance.

"I am," Charlotte wrote Benjamin the next morning, "even more exhausted than you are, and I am really sick with a fever. . . . I have done everything that it was in the power of a human being to do. I have made all the promises that anyone could ask for. Shall I tell you something else? When I think over her violent scenes and all the agony to which I was subjected, I see very clearly that what she really wants is for us to postpone everything. She gave herself away on that point a thousand times over. All right. I can't refuse to do anything that is necessary for our mutual happiness."

But would a delay in the public announcement of their marriage put an end to her anxiety? "It is," she went on, "absolutely essential for us to talk matters over before you see her again. I swore I had no idea where you were staying because I knew she would send someone to get you wherever you were. Let me hear what you want done. The details of our conversation, which lasted six hours, would take too long to write down, and yet you must know everything that passed between us."

Charlotte could not help congratulating herself on her conduct. "I really forced her to show some consideration for me. She did not suffer any convulsions at all in my presence." She did not mention the fact that Germaine was exasperated by her repeating, over and over again, "You see, Benjamin is so kind."

"I feel," Charlotte concluded her letter, "and you must forgive me for uttering this one reproach, that it would have been much better for your happiness and my peace of mind if both of us had kept our freedom rather than have me feel that I owe the tie that binds us only to the very weakness of your character which makes you sorry afterwards."

Back at Coppet on the 13th, Benjamin believed that he might be able to continue playing both his roles if only the public announcement were withheld. "I beg you," he wrote his aunt the Comtesse de Nassau, "to keep everything I am about to tell you to yourself. I have sworn on my word of honor that secrecy will be maintained, and I should not have mentioned this, even to you, my dear aunt, if I did not look upon you as a second self. . . . Keeping faith with an old friendship, and anxious to cause the least possible grief to anyone, I have taken a roundabout course. I have succeeded in what I set out to do, and I am more than recompensed for a few slight inconveniences, when I consider that any other alternative might have done a great deal of harm."

That he was running a certain risk by remaining at Germaine's side did not enter his calculations. He celebrated the 5th of June (the first anniversary of his marriage to Charlotte) by making plans to accompany Germaine to Lyons where the actor Talma was giving another of his superb appearances. Benjamin's anticipation of Talma's performance was keen, so keen that he was not prepared for the histrionics of anyone else. When Charlotte, who had followed Madame de Staël's party to Lyons, presumed to call on her husband at his hotel, she was not received.

The answer to this was inevitable. On the morning of the 9th a note was delivered to Benjamin at his lodgings in the Hôtel du Parc.

"You have abandoned me," wrote Charlotte. "I pity you more than I do myself. I love you. I am, I believe, the only person in the world who has ever truly loved you. The woman responsible for my death is a hard woman, capable of feeling only what she calls humiliation. I have only one last sorrow to savor, which is that of leaving you forever. Pray God that He may forgive me. . . .

"Today I came to the end of my rope. You have abandoned me today, the morning after the day we were married.* My poor dear, I forgive you, although I should have liked to die in your arms. But you could not even do that for me. She wanted me to spend my last hours alone! She took no pity on me in my condition; she takes no pity on anyone. Take pity on yourself if you still love me. Oh, yes, you do love me, but I'll no longer be on hand to hear your voice telling me so. I should have enjoyed that last consolation.

"Your Lotte, your poor Lotte takes you once more into her arms. May the Good Lord bless you and forgive me my sins so that I may find peace after death. Go on living then, and do no harm to anyone, not even to the woman who destroyed me.

* For some curious reason Charlotte made an error of three days.

"I beg you, my dear, take care of all the papers in my secretary. Don't let anyone bury me, my sweet, before you are sure that I'm gone. My God in heaven, now that I am ready, I am in terrible trouble. Can't I see you once more? But come at once. . . ."

This letter, which was opened in Germaine's presence, robbed Benjamin of his presence of mind, at least for that morning. Together they raced to Charlotte's shabby hotel; they found her on a couch, writhing with the poison she had taken, but still alive.

"Unfortunately," Benjamin wrote his aunt later in the day, "you will not be surprised to learn that my plans have been somewhat changed. My wife, who is really an angel, did not want to make a scene which, in spite of myself, might have caused me some trouble. We have however made tremendous strides toward the stability and the calm which are her due and which I long for." As for Germaine, she was all understanding. "The friend whom I desired to hurt as slightly as possible is also good and generous, as much so as might be expected."

A few days later, when Charlotte had begun to recover, Benjamin set off with her on the road to Paris. It was understood that he would return to Coppet for at least three months, once Charlotte had been placed under her physician's care.

For a moment Benjamin may have believed that the scenery could be easily repaired and that he could go on winning his unique success in both his roles. There was no doubt that Germaine was counting on seeing him on the 26th of June, but would she welcome him with her usual commanding indulgence? The letter she wrote Benjamin on the 15th was a warning; she let him know that they would never again be quite so inseparable.

"Thank you for writing me from Roanne," she told him. "It made it possible for me to sleep a few hours, which was something new for me. . . . I thank you for repeating the 26th—I trust you, and from the bottom of my soul I could wish for those three months to be the happy ending of my miserable existence. . . . Now I know that there is one person too many on this earth; no one knows this better than I do. . . . I drag out hours that last as long as days, and everything in the world has died for me—my friends, my children, my thoughts, the sun itself, all these are only shapes which my despair assumes. . . .

"When I see you again, I'll run the risk of believing I've caught hold of life once more! . . . Ah! Benjamin, you have twisted my love for you into a dagger turned against me. So it was on the 8th of June!! * Let's forget about that for a moment. You must have prayed. Pray for me. There was never anyone crippled by this life who needed prayers as much as I do."

Benjamin knew that he would go on seeing Germaine, but as someone else's husband he could not hope to enjoy all of the old anxieties. He had blundered all too quickly into a reality upon which he had never really calculated.

He could of course analyze his disappointment better than anyone else. Even as a boy he had known that he raced for conclusions when he would have done better to pause. "I could wish," he had written his grandmother when he was only twelve, "that someone could stop my blood from circulating so fast. . . . I've tried to see if music could do this for me, I have played adagios and largos that should send thirty cardinals sound asleep, but by some sort of magic these slow tunes end up prestissimo. It's the same thing with dancing. My minuets always end in a gallop. I believe, my dear grandmother, that I am suffering from an incurable disease."

* Germaine was here repeating Charlotte's error.

CHAPTER TWELVE

DE L'ALLEMAGNE

———◆———

IT WAS not so much Benjamin's marriage that Germaine resented as the fact that his foolishness, thanks to Charlotte's indiscretion, was now a matter of public knowledge. "I have suffered horribly by what he has done," she wrote his father more than a year after the attempted suicide. "He has completely destroyed the happiness of my life, for the gift of one's youth should insure the happiness of one's declining years, and there is something terribly cruel about stealing from a woman the years that God has given her with the intention that a friend will keep her company in her old age and down to her very death."

But Germaine could not exist on a diet of rancor. She went on giving herself the pleasure of entertaining Benjamin, even though she could no longer publicly claim him as entirely her own. She also proceeded, knowing that every line she wrote would offend Napoleon, with her projected work on Germany. She was, as Benjamin knew better than anyone else, an indomitable woman.

She was so sure of herself that she could afford to

be foolish on occasion. She contemplated moving to the United States—which was something that no close friend of hers could take seriously. She welcomed, she even overindulged eccentrics. And finally she treated herself to the luxury of something that passed—in the eyes of those who did not know her well—for a genuine love affair.

America was very much on her mind in the summer of 1810, when she rented from Jacques Le Ray the château of Chaumont in the Loire Valley. The château had once sheltered Diane de Poitiers, but the caprices of the Valois kings were less interesting to Germaine than the profits to be made out of real estate in northern New York. Her landlord had invested a sizable sum in that part of the New World and had even founded the village of Leraysville. Germaine herself bought 23,000 acres in St. Lawrence County. To Le Ray she wrote: "I cannot imagine a more noble career than the one you have chosen, and if I weren't bound down by my European habits, I should have the greatest pleasure in becoming an inhabitant of Leraysville."

It was Gouverneur Morris who reminded Germaine that she might be disappointed if she set foot on American soil. "Madame," he told her, "should you ever be seized with a desire for visiting our country, I must inform you beforehand, that your mind will not meet here with the resources which custom has rendered necessary to you. The goodness of your heart will make itself felt everywhere, but there are very few among us who are able to estimate your genius at its real value; in truth we are not worthy of it. It must also be confessed, that whatever self-love may say, we are ignorant of the charms of good French society. We have, however, a little more taste for it than our cold ancestors, the English. Perhaps, too, we are more imaginative and less reasonable."

But Morris could not quench her enthusiasm. If she came, she must not set up too expensive an establishment, he advised her. "Building castles in the air is a diverting folly. Building them in the United States would be a ruinous folly. Labor is too expensive. But to set up a little summer establishment in a new country, which is rapidly advancing; to pass there from three to five months of the fine season; to remain four months more either at Philadelphia or New York, and to spend the remainder of the year traveling; this I consider a mode of life by no means repugnant to common sense."

There came a moment when Morris feared she was actually on her way. "As soon as you arrive," he wrote her, "you will come to Morrisania, partake of what our dairy affords, and refresh yourself. In the beginning of July you shall set out to visit your lands, and the interior country; and return by the middle of September, to repose after your fatigues, to gather peaches, take walks, make verses, romances, in a word to do what you please.

"When my hermitage shall have lost its attractions, you shall establish yourself in the city, where, by the aid of a good cook, you will contrive to live very well. Here, as elsewhere, people amuse themselves with discussions, *bons mots*, slandering their neighbors, and the like."

Morris could not help adding that "you will, perhaps, ridicule a picture in which, among the delights of human life, the form of love does not appear. Well, you have only to give him a place there. . . ."

If Germaine had crossed the ocean, she could hardly have resisted the hospitality of Thomas Jefferson, even though Gouverneur Morris would have done his best to dissuade her from visiting the White House when anyone but a Federalist was in office. To all such advice Germaine would have paid no attention; she was an unqualified admirer of the great democrat of the New World, and she wrote him more than once to insist on her loyalty to his principles. "Your name," she informed the President, "is sacred in France. Even if it is never uttered in public, in private it is uttered again and again, and if in a low voice, that's because one's conscience always speaks softly." She added that her older son Auguste might come to the United States the following year to look into his mother's investments.

Jefferson, who understood that his answer might fall into the hands of Napoleon's police, hesitated to put into writing any endorsement of her stand against the Emperor. "Unmeddling with the affairs of other nations," he sagaciously began, "we presume not to prescribe or censure their course." Then he went on to recall the pleasant reception Germaine's father had given him in Paris. "The grandson of Monsieur Necker cannot fail of a healthy welcome in a country which so much respected him. He will find a sincere welcome at Monticello."

Auguste never made the trip, possibly because his mother could not spare him from Chaumont. There were many guests at the château; to watch over them, to please them required a retinue. Perhaps the most important of all was Juliette Récamier. "The last time I saw you," Germaine wrote Juliette shortly before her arrival in the Loire Valley, "I was drawn to you as I have never been to any other woman in my life. How can it be that you are so attractive to me?" She added: "Perhaps you would like to know what is going on with Benjamin and me. Our minds are in closer contact than ever. But since we no longer spend our days quarreling, our souls scarcely touch, and each of us suffers in his own fashion, but alone."

Benjamin, of course, could not keep away from Chaumont. He slipped free from Charlotte for seven weeks, time enough for him to judge the world in which Germaine was moving without his supervision. Prosper de Barante turned up, as did his father. So did Mathieu de Montmorency. And while Miss Randall, Germaine's English secretary, was watching over the household details, August Wilhelm von Schlegel was there to give any advice that was needed on the manuscript dealing with Germany.

But Schlegel was not the only German in Germaine's entourage. Adelbert von Chamisso, who had not yet written *Peter Schlemihl*, the unforgettable if not exactly immortal story of the man who sold his shadow, made himself almost completely at home in the château. Almost but not quite. Miss Randall (whom Chamisso referred to as "my porcupiney enemy from the British Isles") had the room next to his, and insisted that he smoke his pipe out of doors.

By way of compensation Chamisso gazed at the Loire Valley and found the view superb from the Gothic towers. And even if Miss Randall was round as a barrel, besides being cold and harsh as far as his pipe was concerned, and even if Schlegel was a trifle too cool, too clever, and too melancholy for his taste, he much admired the saintly Mathieu de Montmorency, and looked with something like longing on Juliette Récamier.

As for Germaine, she was someone else. "What a strange being she is!" he wrote his friend Friedrich Heinrich Karl de la Motte-Fouqué, who was on the eve of publishing *Undine*. "She has all the earnestness of a German, the warmth of a southerner, and the feeling for form of a Frenchwoman. She is sincere, she never hides her feelings, she is a passionate soul (she can be jealous)—she is enthusiasm personified. . . . Music is everything for her, she lives only to listen, music must be around her at all times, especially when she is writing, and as a matter of fact, she writes only music. . . . It's only the geometry of life that she fails to comprehend."

Chamisso was flattered that she had taken him up, recognized his talents, and bestowed her confidence upon him. Far from being provoked, he was amused when Germaine, deep in her work on Germany, decreed that not a word was to be spoken in her drawing room. Her guests, for want of any other means of communication, took to writing each other little notes which they passed across the great round table. This letter writing —*la petite poste* he called it—often led to explanations which the guests were able to pronounce out loud in the gardens. Schlegel, who kept gloomily to his own room, was the only one who never joined the group in the silent hall.

So Germaine suffered no interruptions that summer as she studied the galleys of her manuscript on Germany. She was only slightly inconvenienced when her landlord unexpectedly returned from a visit to the United States. He begged her to stay on, but rather than put him to any trouble, she moved to the neighboring château of Fossé, lent her by its owner Monsieur de Salaberry. At Fossé she thought, as any author should, only of the ordeal of correcting proof.

As early as the 8th of February, 1810, she had signed a contract with H. Nicolle in Paris, whereby she received 13,000 francs for her three-volume work, and a credit in addition of 2,400 francs in the publisher's bookstore. All seemed to be going smoothly as the summer advanced. When Nicolle wrote her on the 2nd of September in regard to certain changes insisted upon by the imperial censors, he was not particularly concerned, and neither, one would guess, was Germaine, even though she was obliged to delete a reference to a Chinese wall around France, to moderate her praise of Prince Ferdinand of Prussia, and to alter a passage in which she pointed out that good taste in literature was like peace and quiet under a despotism—the important thing was the price paid for it. On the 23rd of September Germaine gave the publisher her *bon à tirer*, or the right to proceed with the printing, and there was every reason to expect that the book would shortly go on sale.

But if Germaine so believed, she was careless. On June 3, 1810, Fouché had been replaced as Napoleon's Minister of Police by Anne-Jean-Marie-René Savary, Duc de Rovigo. This was ominous. Germaine could always hope to appeal to Fouché, for all his faults. The Duc de Rovigo could be moved by no man's tears. As Napoleon himself observed: "If I ordered Savary to do away with his wife and children, I am sure he would not hesitate for a second." He had proved a shrewd ambassador for the Empire in both Saint Petersburg and Madrid, but his greatest service was rendered at the time of the supposed conspiracy of the Duc d'Enghien. Savary was in command of the troops at Vincennes on the day the Duc d'Enghien was executed—or assassinated.

With Savary Napoleon felt that he could discuss the problem of Germaine without the slightest anxiety. "I have returned Madame de Staël's work to you," he reported to the Minister of Police on September 28. "Has she really the right to call herself a baroness? . . . Suppress the passage about the Duke of Brunswick, and three fourths of the passages where she makes so much of England. That unfortunate infatuation of hers has already done us harm enough."

Here the Emperor was talking like a moderately angry man. He grew more angry when he learned that young Auguste de Staël had come to Paris to request permission for his mother to live at only forty leagues' distance from the capital. And he was furious when he examined Germaine's own letter.

184

"Your Majesty has been informed," she wrote, "that I missed Paris only because of the museums and of Talma's acting. That is an amusing joke about being sent into exile—in other words about the misfortune that Cicero and Bolingbroke declared to be the greatest of all. But even if I did love the masterpieces of art which France owes to the conquests of Your Majesty, even if I loved those great tragedies, those invitations to heroism, could you, Sire, blame me for that? You surely would agree that the happiness of every individual is based on the nature of his capacities. And if God has bestowed any talents on me, would you deny that I have the kind of imagination which makes the enjoyment of art and the appreciation of the intellect an absolute necessity? So many people ask Your Majesty for favors of all kinds that I see no reason why I should blush to ask you for the gift of friendship—for poetry, music, and pictures—for that ideal existence that I cannot share without the reverence due the ruler of France."

An abject letter might have pleased the Emperor, but not a communication of this sort in which the pride of the daughter of Necker was evident. The audience that Germaine prayed for was never given. And when Juliette Récamier sought to use her influence with the Director of Censorship—who happened to be an accomplice of Savary—the end was near.

On September 25 the police descended on Nicolle; every copy that had been run off the presses was seized, and so were the plates. On the 27th the prefect of Loir-et-Cher, Monsieur de Corbigny, who had often enjoyed Germaine's hospitality, showed up at Fossé. His orders were to confiscate the last sheet of proof and the least scrap of manuscript. He also had the embarrassing duty to inform her that she must leave France immediately, either for Coppet or for an American port. But Corbigny arrived too late to carry out the first of his orders. Germaine could offer the prefect only a fragment of her work; proof and manuscript had already been handed to young Albert de Staël, who scrambled over the garden wall with the treasure. He handed it in turn to August Wilhelm von Schlegel, who was to race to Vienna and confide it to the safekeeping of his brother Friedrich.

As late as the 29th of September Germaine could still hope that the book might be published, even if in mutilated form. The censors issued a favorable report on the third volume. But her hopes were shattered. On the 11th of October the plates were smashed by the police, and Nicolle was forced into bankruptcy. "Your latest work," the Duc de Rovigo notified Germaine, "is not French. . . . I have had the impression that the climate of this country does not suit you, and you must know that we have no idea of modeling our civilization on that of the nations you admire." He added: "Although my predecessor allowed you to live in the Department of Loir-et-Cher, you must not think that his tolerance rescinded the instructions that have been drawn up for your case."

Germaine understood that there was no alternative to Coppet. Before October was over she and Schlegel were back in her father's villa. In the meantime Chateaubriand had made the cause of the bankrupt Nicolle his own. "Do you know, my dear lady," the poet addressed the author of *De l'Allemagne*, "that there is a certain black bird who shows himself at sea on the eve of shipwrecks? While geese and ducks and other birds seek safety on the ground, this black bird follows after the vessel that is lashed by the winds. I cannot speak for the birds. So I keep silent and listen to the prudent goslings who have flown home. In spite of all this nonsense you will understand that I have shared your grief; that is the most important thing of all.

"I am writing you from my retreat. I have a little cottage at three leagues from Paris. But even a cottage is too good for me. If, like you, I had an admirable château on the edge of Lake Geneva, I should never leave it. The public would never read a line of mine. I should take as much trouble to make myself forgotten as I have taken to make myself known. And you, my dear lady, why the very thing that would make me happy makes you very unhappy indeed. Such is the heart of a man."

This was an appeal which could not be resisted; Germaine refunded Nicolle not only the 13,000 francs he had offered for her book, but also the credit he had given her at his bookshop.

Desperate herself, Germaine made a point at this time of entertaining at Coppet two of the most frantic individuals at liberty in Europe, the poet Zacharias Werner and the novelist Julie de Krüdener. Goethe shuddered at the ecstasies of Werner's dramas, but Germaine bravely encouraged the delirium that swept him into the Roman Catholic Church. "I am singularly attached to him," she confessed to the Grand Duchess of Weimar. "Such a unity of intellect and soul . . . is almost unique, and how much delicacy with his strength. I wish he would renounce his systems on the stage, but I like them in private. If there is any man who can make up for the loss of Schiller, it is he."

She even forgave Werner for suggesting that she did not treat Schlegel with all the respect that was his due. "Excuse me," he once wrote her, "my lovely friend, my conscience forces me to add a word or two about our worthy friend, my fellow countryman A. W. S. You know of course that this man, possibly the noblest character of all German men of letters, is absolutely devoted to you. However, he is the only man whom you—you, the very personification of generosity in his eyes—whom you deal with in a way which does not live up to your usual magnanimity. The health of A. W. S. is as fragile and delicate as his life is precious to the world at large."

It was Werner's hope that Germaine would find peace as he had in the bosom of the Roman Catholic Church. "I tremble for my own life after death," he reminded her, "but I tremble also at the thought of yours. Let me kiss your knees, I beg you, my sister, my benefactress. I implore you, and my eyes swell with tears. Seek grace in the only place where it may be bestowed, in the heart of the church. I fall down before you (oh, how cold the expression is!), I beg of you, I implore you, I shriek out my prayer (alas, why can't my shrieks reach the depths of your soul?), become a CATHOLIC this very second!"

There was, of course, a touch of the heretic in this violent Roman Catholic; this was doubtless the secret of his success at Coppet. "Do you know what it is that one loves in one's mistress?" Werner asked another guest at the château. "It is God." He did not become a Roman Catholic priest until he had made the most of three marriages.

Werner's dramas (Germaine could not always guess the future reputation of an author) are rarely if ever performed in the twentieth century. Even *The Twenty-fourth of February*, which shocked audiences of 150 years ago, is not accorded the respect given Schiller, Hauptmann, or Brecht. This is unfortunate; it would be interesting to discover the response of our time to a play based on the murder of a homecoming son (traveling in disguise) by his greedy father and mother.

The fiction of Baroness Julie de Krüdener (née Barbara Juliana von Vietinghof) is even less appreciated than the plays of Werner. This, too, may be a reflection on our taste. Her *Valérie*, the tale of the hopeless love of young Gustave de Linar for the child-bride of a count whom he served as secretary, is a delightful reminder of the days when the sales of novels were in direct proportion to the tears shed by readers. But if *Valérie* is forgotten—like so many other books inspired by Julie de Krüdener's friend Bernardin de Saint-Pierre —the Baroness will live forever in history thanks to the influence she exerted on Tsar Alexander I of Russia. She was pursuing him at the time he was laying his plans for the Holy Alliance. "The Lord will give me the pleasure of seeing him," she assured a friend, and she did see him again and again. "You are still in your sins," was her first word to the Tsar. "The life of Christ must circulate morally through your spiritual body."

Although Lord Castlereagh was of the opinion that Julie de Krüdener was simply "an old fanatic who has a considerable reputation among the few high-fliers in religion that are to be found in Paris," there were those who took her seriously. She was not free of her husband (the Russian ambassador to Venice and Copenhagen) until his death in 1801; it was then that her real career began. Returning to her native Riga, she became a convert to the Moravian Brethren; this conversion set her on a quest to meet every mystical reformer in Europe. She drew close to Johann Adam Müller, a peasant who suffered from visions. She sat at the feet of the dark-minded preacher Johann-Heinrich Jüng-Stilling at the court of Baden. And at Sainte-Marie-aux-Mines in Alsace she sought out Pastor Fontaine and his hysterical disciple Marie Kummer.

Germaine was impressed by Julie, or perhaps we should say that she was entertained. "I thought her distinguished," the mistress of Coppet remarked, "but she tells so many stories of men who have killed themselves for love of her that her conversation gives the impression of being a wager." Not all of Germaine's guests were so considerate. Charles-Victor de Bonstetten, a Swiss who had pondered long on the moral influence of northern climates, was actually annoyed by the behavior of this northern specimen. "Krüdener has just flown through," he reported to a friend. "She is quite mad and spoke to Madame de Staël of heaven and hell. To me such excesses reek like asafetida, but if one does not go too near, these people are amusing."

In the end Germaine was benevolent. "She is certainly changed in heart," she said of Julie de Krüdener. "Her religion has touched me." The author of *Valérie* was equally kind. "We must abandon Madame de Staël to God," she declared. "She cannot escape from Him."

Shortly after these courtesies were exchanged—early in 1811, to be exact—Germaine conceived a passion of such intensity that she could pay less than the usual attention to her guests. Her intellect was not touched in this instance, which was not surprising. Her mind had been sharpened by Benjamin Constant.

Albert-Michel-Jean (or John) Rocca was the man who inspired this interest. "I'll love her so much that she'll have to marry me," was his first observation. A veteran of the French invasion of Spain, he was still hobbling on crutches he used while recovering from a wound he had suffered at Ronda. He was twenty-three when they met. She was forty-four.

"When I came into the ballroom," he recalled, "I could see no one but her, and thinking that everyone could tell that I had fallen in love with her, I moved away from where she was standing so that I could gaze upon her more at my ease. Whenever I drew near to speak to her, I began blushing, I turned pale, and I made one blunder after another trying to pay her the kind of compliments that other people were distributing so easily. My embarrassment was my only eloquence."

August Wilhelm von Schlegel, who could not help

observing that the mistress of Coppet was enchanted by this new admirer, was deeply troubled. "I have an awful headache," he wrote Germaine one afternoon, "and I should like you to excuse me from lunch. Whatever you may think about my state of mind, I know very well that what distresses me is the shock of discovering in a soul as beautiful as yours the unmistakable evidence of a frivolity which destroys any confidence in your friendship. Just think of the situation of a man whose whole life depends on this claim to your friendship, and who occupies such an inferior position in your soul that you run the risk of sacrificing him for a silly flirtation! At a time when I have the opportunity of carrying out all kinds of projects, and not following in your train, you have formed an attachment which might banish me forever, and this after having labored seven years under a misconception. You not only have this idea in the back of your mind, but you have talked about it to the man who is the unworthy object of your affection, and you have granted him certain inalienable rights.

"Every evening, locked up in my room," August Wilhelm concluded, "I might as well be in a dungeon, for people are strolling to and fro in front of my door, making fun of the plight I am in."

Schlegel was, after all, a friend. Germaine had her enemies, and they could not pass up the opportunity of making uncharitable comments on the progress of this new passion. The most vindictive of all observers was the Comtesse de Boigne, who had never forgiven the mistress of Coppet for arriving three hours late for a dinner party in Geneva. What was even worse, in Madame de Boigne's opinion, was that Germaine made a point, once she was on the scene, of chatting only with the friends she had brought in her train.

The Comtesse was also distressed by certain remarks her rival let drop in the presence of one of Napoleon's prefects. "I am," said Germaine, "generally satisfied with the performance of servants in his station." Madame de Boigne was particularly displeased, however, by her acting in the part of mother. Coming upon little Albertine in tears, the Comtesse asked what was the matter. "Alas," Albertine replied, "people think that I am happy, but there is a chasm in my heart." Was this pure affectation? So it seemed to this onlooker. "She was only eleven," Madame de Boigne remarked in her memoirs, "but she was already talking Coppet."

Germaine's infatuation for Rocca offered an even choicer opportunity for malice; in her reminiscences the Comtesse dwelled with obvious delight on an evening when the lady from Coppet had asked her to sing a few songs. She sang, but she listened to much besides the sound of her own voice. At the end of the concert up came Rocca on his crutches to stammer out a few words of embarrassment and praise. His confusion, so it seemed, was too much for his mistress. "Ah," sighed Germaine, "speech is not his language."

It was cruel of Madame de Boigne to recall the wit of her enemy on this occasion. On the 7th of April, 1812, Germaine was delivered of a little boy whose father was Rocca. Baptized Louis-Alphonse Giles, the "son" of Theodore Giles of Boston, Massachusettes, and Henriette Preston, his head was too large for his body, his eyes were timid, and his stammer grew more and more pronounced. It was obvious that he was mentally retarded and would never enjoy anything in all his life quite so much as the squirrel (wound up with a key) with which he was presented as an infant.

The birth of the child could not be concealed from Napoleon's agents in Geneva. "The dropsy of Madame de Staël has fortunately disappeared," came the report to the Duc de Rovigo's desk. "The end product of her illness is a boy. . . . Her marvelous recovery has been attributed to a Genevan by the name of Rocca." Nor was Benjamin Constant unaware of what was going on. "Could Madame de Staël be pregnant?" he asked his diary in the spring of 1812. Long before this, Rocca had been so concerned over a visit of his to Geneva that he challenged him to a duel. Benjamin drew a will the second he was provoked, but the meeting on the field of honor never took place. Germaine, who was more alarmed than either of her lovers, insisted that she would not allow the father of Albertine to be killed.

It was not until the 10th of October, 1816, that Germaine and Rocca were married by a pastor; by that time the little boy—whom they always called "Petit Nous"— was a hopeless case. To anyone as sensitive as his mother, his pitiful condition must have been a visible sign that there was a curse on passion when the intellect was not involved.

But in the meantime Napoleon had intervened once more. Monsieur Capelle, his new prefect in Geneva, was so indelicate in the spring of 1812 as to ask the author of *Corinne* to write a hymn in honor of Napoleon's heir, the Prince of Rome. This was more than she could contemplate. Shortly thereafter she ventured to Aix-en-Savoie for a few days at a thermal establishment. She had not been there a fortnight when she was ordered to return to Coppet. Then came the command that she must not stray more than two leagues from her father's house.

And on the very same day that she was thus restricted, Schlegel was ordered out of Geneva and Coppet. His preference for Euripides' *Phaedra* over that of Racine was irritating the authorities in Paris. "It was," Germaine decided, "rather refined of a Corsican monarch to make so much of the standards of French literature. But to tell the truth, Schlegel was sent into exile because he was my friend and his conversation cheered my lonely days. They were plotting to make my mind a prison to me by robbing me of all the pleasures of the intellect and of all my friends."

One threat followed another. Mathieu de Montmorency found he was banned from France for daring to visit Coppet. Juliette Récamier, braving Germaine's warnings, was welcomed with tears at the entrance to the château, but even she understood that she could not stay near her dear friend. Juliette fled the next day; this was not soon enough for the Emperor, who exiled her for her audacity. It was evident that anyone who visited Germaine would be harassed by the French government. One friend explained to Germaine: "If you stay, he'll treat you like Mary Stuart: nineteen years of misery, and then the end."

At last, on the 23rd of May, 1812, Germaine gathered Auguste, Albertine, and Rocca into her carriage and set off on what appeared to be an afternoon's drive. She carried a fan, as did her daughter, and they left word they would be back for dinner. "Just imagine that you're on your way to England," Albertine remarked; she knew that Sweden was their destination. Albert was to join them later on; "Petit Nous" was left behind in the care of a pastor.

Near Bern they met Schlegel, who was waiting for his patroness in a barn; they raced on, arriving in Vienna on the 6th of June, and there Germaine began to realize that for a famous woman there were untold anxieties in a life of exile. The farther she traveled from her father's house, the more dependent she was on those who had chosen to follow in her train. She trembled lest Rocca and Schlegel quarrel in public.

"I've told him all about my feeling for you," Germaine carefully informed the father of "Petit Nous," "for I did not want anything to disturb my love for you, which must last as long as I live."

She also had to take into consideration the point of view of her children. "Auguste," she pointed out to Rocca, "has asked us not to appear in public together in Vienna. You'll have to use your head . . . we'll have to plan some way of seeing each other at least twice a day, for I could easily imagine I'd never see you again if I didn't see you constantly." The advice was well meant, but it was unnerving to her lover, who lived in dread that he could be taken for a gigolo. "This trip we are taking," she reminded him, "is the most magnificent proof of your devotion to me."

Germaine had her troubles with Albertine, too. Her daughter was fond of Rocca, she called him Caliban, and she got him to give her English lessons, but she had her suspicions that her mother had formed an attachment. "I used to go around singing a gay tune even though I was terribly depressed," Albertine put down in her diary. "I thought there were any number of advantages to being young, and that I'd never enjoy any of them. . . . I was terribly worried about something in the back of my mind about R. . . . I had decided that this thought of mine would not have any effect upon my conduct, but I did not have the strength of character which comes from saying outright what one thinks to a person whom one is very close to. . . . Finally, God gave his blessing, and from that moment on I was calm and tranquil and I got that idea out of my head."

Little Albertine had more than respect for her mother. "The idea I have formed of her," she confessed to her diary, "cannot be separated in my soul from the idea of God. All of my self-esteem is bound up in her. . . . It sometimes happens that I stare at Mama a whole hour long, hoping she'll guess what I've been thinking, for I can't possibly express it in words. How can one ever define the feelings of a daughter for her mother?

They say it's a very simple matter, but I know I feel something about her which is very far from being as simple as that." At this time she knew nothing whatever about the birth of "Petit Nous."

But these were not the only worries of Germaine on her way to Sweden. There was that painful evening in the castle of Lanzut in Poland, when Prince Lubomirski did his best to bid her welcome, but a policeman made his appearance and told Auguste that "out of delicacy" he would refrain from sleeping in her room to watch over her. Her son then said that he would throw him out the window if he made the attempt, and the party left the castle rather than cause the prince any inconvenience with the authorities.

There were, of course, occasional compensations. When she reached Russia she was welcomed by a man who had been a clerk in her father's office; his eyes filled with tears. Then General Miloradowitsch was so courteous in Kiev that Germaine felt that she stood "at the gate to another world, near the East from which have come so many religious beliefs, and in whose sanctuary are to be discovered incredible treasures of perseverance and reflection." And at Saint Petersburg she saw the British flag floating over the Neva, a symbol of freedom in her eyes. Count Orlof asked her to spend the day on the island bearing his name, Count Romanzov introduced her to the British ambassador, and both the Tsar and the Tsarina received her with dignity and kindness.

At Saint Catherine's Institute one of the young girls was so polite as to recite a few passages from her father's *Cours de Morale Religieuse*. That was a moving experience. So was the day she spent in the country with Narischkin, the Chamberlain of the Court. Moscow was in ruins, but Napoleon was retreating, and Narischkin proposed a toast to the victory of Russia and England. "They were all drunk with hope," Germaine recalled, "and my eyes filled with tears. Was it possible for a foreign tyrant to lead me to the point of wishing for the defeat of France?"

"I drink," said Germaine, "to the downfall of the man who has overrun France and Europe. For the day on which he is defeated will be a victory for all real Frenchmen." She noted that her toast was approved by Narischkin, and in fact by all of the English and Russians present, and that "the name of France . . . was received with benevolence by the knights of the East and of the sea."

This was comforting, but Germaine was horror-stricken when Rocca and Albert returned from an evening at the theater with the report that *Phèdre* had been hissed. "The barbarians!" Germaine cried out as she broke into tears. "Think of not wanting to listen to Racine's *Phèdre!*"

At last, at the end of September, she left Saint Petersburg for Finland and Sweden. Napoleon's ex-general Bernadotte was, she discovered, the real hero of the century, and Schlegel immediately went to work on a pamphlet devoted to his cause. This was an admirable endeavor which Germaine encouraged, but she could not forget Benjamin, even with Schlegel and Rocca at her side. More than once Rocca surprised her with tears in her eyes reading Constant's letters.

"For the last two months I haven't had a word from you," she wrote Benjamin from Stockholm on the 20th of May, 1813, "and for two years now I haven't seen you. Do you remember the promise we made that we should never be separated from each other? . . . I must tell you that you have missed your chance for a great career, not to mention everything else. . . . And what in the world will happen to me, isolated as I am? Whom can I talk to, and who will stand by me? . . .

My father, you, and Mathieu will always have their claims upon my heart."

In the next month she set sail for England, leaving Albert in Schlegel's care, and for perhaps the first time in her wanderings felt the warmth of triumph rather than the sting of exile. She had been famous wherever she went; in London she was more than welcome.

While Benjamin, stopping in Brunswick, was reviewing his feelings for Charlotte—"I love her, but in contemplating her affection, I think of that of Madame de Staël for me, and I am tortured by memories of her and Albertine," he confided to his diary—Germaine was making the conquest of Lord Byron.

"Although," she wrote the poet, "you make the mistake of despising mankind, it seems to me that mankind is doing all it can to make up to you, and that fate has not been unkind to the man who has become the first poet of the century. . . . Please be a little more kind to those who admire you, and be thankful that I've forgiven you, as a genius, all the things I don't like about you. I should like to have a talk with you. When shall I be found worthy of such an opportunity?"

Byron was quickly impressed. So was the Duchess of Devonshire, and so was Tom Moore who wrote his mother that "I find I am a great favorite with this celebrated Madame de Staël that has lately arrived and is making such a noise in London: she says she has a *passion* for my poetry."

As for Sir James Mackintosh, the Scot who answered Burke's slurs on the French Revolution, he was so taken with Germaine that he momentarily abandoned his labors on what was to become the *Progress of Ethical Philosophy*. His presence at tea was, however, resented by Rocca with whom she had to reason constantly at the height of the London season.

"I can't begin to understand the way you're acting,"

she told him after he refused to take Sir James's hand. "You'll soon find out what the consequences are in this country! My daughter and I bitterly resent what happened, and there was never a scene made by anyone that was more cruel or more inopportune. . . . Sir James is the most literary connection I could think of, and a highly advisable connection in my circumstances."

Wisely, Germaine had exiled Rocca to Bath for the first few weeks of her stay in England. He could easily be awkward; of that she was well aware when she wrote Benjamin that her new lover would behave as discreetly as Mathieu de Montmorency. Yet she went on to protest that Rocca "has stood by me in my misfortunes with a generosity and a warmth of heart that I shall never forget. He is quite changed, and you would recognize neither his manners nor his conversation."

Possibly Benjamin forgave her those lines. If she was overwrought, there was a reason. One evening on returning from the opera, Germaine got word from Schlegel that Albert had been killed in a duel with a Russian officer at Doberan on the Baltic.

Germaine had not quite recovered from this loss when she ventured to find fault with a letter of Benjamin in which he expressed the hope that Napoleon would be eliminated by the Russians. "What free spirit," she exploded, "could hope that he would be defeated by the Cossacks!"

She grew even angrier when she learned that Benjamin was proposing that France be placed in quarantine once the allies were victorious. "I have read your memorandum," she announced. "May God preserve me from ever showing it to anybody. I shall do nothing against France. In the hour of her misfortune I shall turn against her neither my reputation (which I owe to her) nor the name of my father (whom she loved)." She could not forget that the villages to which the invaders were setting fire lay along the road where women once threw themselves on their knees to watch Necker pass. "You are not French, Benjamin," she concluded.

She could be severe with her old friend, but she could not conceive of abandoning him. She no sooner reached Paris on the 12th of May, 1814, ten days after the return of Louis XVIII, than she got in touch with Benjamin, eager to enlighten him. On the 19th of June he and Lord Wellington dined with her, and it is more than likely that she reviewed in their company the future of France.

She could speak with a certain authority on almost any subject that claimed her attention. In October, 1813, one of the great ambitions of her life had been gratified: John Murray published the work on Germany to which she had dedicated so many years. It was an instant success; the first printing was exhausted in three days. A German translation was available as early as April of the next year; in May Nicolle issued the book in France.

One hundred fifty years later *De l'Allemagne* remains one of the most eloquent advertisements ever written of a foreign land. Unlike De Toqueville's observations on America, it is not a work of prophecy. Germaine did not foresee—why should she?— that the Germany of Goethe and Schiller would be corrupted by the nationalism of Arndt and Jahn. Her achievement was to remind the world of German literature at the very time when German poets were challenging those of ancient and established languages.

And although Heinrich Heine liked to believe that she was merely the echo of August Wilhelm von Schlegel, the truth is that she spoke for herself.* She made her mistakes. She was not a musician, and her com-

* Germaine's descendant, the Comtesse Jean de Pange, has demolished this myth in *Auguste-Wilhelm Schlegel et Madame de Staël.*

ments on German music are naïve. She thought, for instance, that Mozart's *Requiem* was "not sufficiently solemn for the occasion"; she decided that Haydn was too intellectual for his own good; and she did not mention Beethoven. Nor was Germaine a critic of architecture in any sense of the word. Although she crossed the Rhine in the age of Schinkel and Persius, she declared there was no modern architecture worth looking at, and she was so innocent of any knowledge concerning Balthasar Neumann and the other great architects of the eighteenth century that she claimed that the only monuments of importance dated from the Middle Ages.

Mistakes she made, but she was not blind to German faults. "The love of liberty," she realized, "is far from being encouraged." She added that "the great minds of Germany will indulge in the most violent arguments concerning the world of ideas, and won't allow anyone to interfere with their speculations, but so far as the real world goes, they are only too eager to submit to authority." She admitted that the Germans had always respected women—while the French had done their best to be agreeable to them.

"There is," she felt, "no country in which there is a more vital need for literature than Germany. Since the social world has nothing to offer, and individuals lack the grace and vivacity that come naturally in warm climates, the result is that Germans are charming only when they feel important, and that only geniuses can afford to be clever."

She knew that "a Frenchman always has something to say, even when he has no ideas at all, while a German always has more ideas in his head than he knows how to express." As for the art of telling a story, this was unknown on the other side of the Rhine. "Audiences are far too easy to please, and bores are given too many opportunities. The people who try to tell stories rely too heavily on the patience of their listeners."

She agreed that "Germans give the necessary time to everything they set out to accomplish, but what is necessary, as far as conversation is concerned, is to be amusing. If that point is overlooked, there is always the danger of launching into a discussion or a serious review of the question at hand—a useful occupation rather than a delightful art."

She never lost her sense of humor, even though her extensive survey of German literature ranged from the *Nibelungenlied* to the works of her exact contemporaries. She was incisive—she was probably accurate—when she held that Goethe's dramas might be considered from two points of view. "In the plays he has written with the stage in mind, there is a great deal of grace and wit, but nothing else. On the other hand he has displayed an extraordinary talent in those of his plays which are almost impossible to perform. It would seem that the genius of Goethe cannot be confined by the limits of a theater."

She was deeply moved by his *Iphigenie*, the one work in which he hinted at the glacial perfection of Racine. And when she complained that *Faust* (she was referring to Part I) could not be taken as a model, she was penetrating, coming as she did from a civilization in which literature has always been based on models. Whether or not *Faust* was fit to be imitated, it had its virtues. "Such a composition," she reasoned, "should be judged like a dream. If good taste," she went on, "were always on guard at the ivory gates to the dream world, forcing our fancies into a familiar pattern, our dreams would only rarely strike the imagination."

Germaine was a perceptive critic, and quotation after quotation might be cited to prove that *De l'Allemagne* was an irresistible invitation to explore the literature of Germany. This indeed it was, and it is probable that

Gérard de Nerval might never have published his translation of *Faust* without her example. Yet it would be foolish to argue that her work exerted a direct influence on French literature. The great French romantics owed very little to the romantics of Germany; Baudelaire, for example, was not inspired by Novalis. But Germaine's influence was all the greater for being indirect. Her gallant questioning of the authority of the French classics may well have contributed to the quest of the romantic generation for classics other than those which were so well established, and it is likely that Ronsard might not have been rediscovered in the romantic period if she had not stirred the atmosphere.

"We have not, I imagine," she set down at the very beginning of *De l'Allemagne*, "come to the point where we wish to erect a Chinese wall around French literature in order to prevent ideas coming in from the outside world." This was a direct challenge to the dictatorship of Napoleon. The fact that it sent a generation in search of new precedents in the French past could not have displeased her.

No romantic could remain indifferent to the hymn to enthusiasm with which she ended her great work. She explained that the meaning of the word enthusiasm was *god in us*.

CHAPTER THIRTEEN

"I HAVE ALWAYS BEEN THE SAME . . ."

GERMAINE, who had never been noted for her discretion, saw no reason why the author of *De l'Allemagne* should sink into comfortable obscurity. When Napoleon landed on the morning of March 6, 1815, she had the wit to perceive that his bid to reconquer France and Europe might be successful, and she set out at once for the safety of Coppet. But security had never been attractive to her, and she spent a good many hours wondering what advantage she might derive from this sudden change in the political atmosphere.

"Liberty is now lost forever!" was her first thought when Napoleon set foot on French soil. "He hates me, he hates every trait that I have inherited from my father, he hates my friends, he hates all of our ideas, he hates the spirit of 1789."

But on second thought she decided that she might resume her previous friendly relations with Napoleon's family. She had always been fond of Joseph, the one-time king of Spain. Now she was suddenly interested in the career of Napoleon's brother-in-law Murat, who had been king of Naples. "I worship you," she wrote

Murat three days after Napoleon landed, "not because you are a king, not because you are a hero, but because you are a real friend of liberty."

This letter was to prove an embarrassing document when Waterloo silenced the last pretensions of the Emperor. All of her correspondence with Murat passed into the hands of Louis XVIII, who gave one of his ministers the pleasure of returning every letter to her. "Madame," the minister announced, "you may continue to write letters and receive answers. You may travel in France, you may travel outside of France, you may come back to France, and you may live here. We place so little importance on what you do, or say, or write, that the government has no interest in learning what you are up to. Nor will the government interfere with you in any way, nor allow anyone to give you a second's uneasiness in regard to any of your plans or your secrets."

This was an awkward moment, made doubly so by the fact that she suspected that the king was well aware of her solicitude for Napoleon when he was still on Elba. Germaine had heard of a plot to murder the Emperor; in her anxiety to save his life, she rushed to Joseph at his country home and proposed that she, with the actor Talma who happened to be Joseph's guest at the time, set off that very second to warn her old enemy of the danger he was in. In the end another messenger was selected, but this extenuating circumstance could not have charmed Louis XVIII.

Germaine's only consolation, if consoled she could be, was that Napoleon, for the hundred days in which he was suffered on the continent of Europe, was inclined to a new leniency. "I made a mistake," he confessed to his brother Lucien. "Madame de Staël made more enemies for me in exile than she would have made in France."

In the meantime Benjamin had been his usual unquiet self; after astonishing all of his old friends by displaying the most perfect prudence, he succeeded in damaging his political career by the most imprudent gesture of his life.

Early in 1814 he had the good sense to publish in Hanover a pamphlet on the spirit of conquest which attracted, deservedly, the attention of opinion-makers everywhere on the eve of Napoleon's downfall. A conscientious attack on the Emperor's methods, *De l'esprit de conquête* reminded the civilized world that all tyranny was impermanent. "The despotism of France," he claimed, "has hunted down the spirit of liberty from coast to coast; for a time it was stifled in every land that France had overrun. But since the spirit of liberty has kept on finding new hiding places, despotism has extended itself so far that it has come to its proper end. The genius of mankind was lying in wait at the outer limits of the globe, to make sure that if despotism showed itself again it would be recognized as a shameful thing, and be punished in memorable fashion."

These were wise words, but written by an ambitious man. When Bernadotte, on whom he had been betting, returned to Stockholm rather than try for the crown of France, Benjamin began to consider what might be done with Louis XVIII. He called on Talleyrand, who was about to begin a new career as the adviser of Napoleon's successor; he dashed off three admirable pamphlets in which he went into laudable detail on the subject of constitutional monarchy, speaking up for trial by jury, religious tolerance, and freedom of the press.

All this was before Napoleon's landing. Benjamin's first reaction to the news was to compose an article for the *Journal de Paris* in which he pointed out that the Emperor was no better than a coward. "My article for tomorrow's newspaper has put my life in danger," he noted, with the proper pride, in his diary. *"Vogue la galère*. If all is lost, let's go down gracefully. What cowards those diehard loyalists are. . . . They are trembling from head to foot, and I am the only man who has dared to stand up."

As Napoleon drew nearer Paris, Benjamin became even more eloquent. On the 19th of March he made his position plain in the *Journal des Débats*. "I have always been the champion of liberty," he announced. "I am not the man to crawl like a miserable turncoat, from one despot to another."

It was on the next morning that Napoleon re-entered the capital. "The king has gone," Benjamin reported to his diary. "Collapse, and universal cowardice." He himself left the city on the 21st. But by the night of the 27th he was making his way back to Paris from Sèvres.

And on the 30th Benjamin took the liberty of calling on Joseph Bonaparte. "I have my hopes," he told his diary. "Possibly liberty can be preserved." On the 14th of April he was received by the Emperor. "Long conversation," he jotted down in his notebook. "He is a remarkable man. Tomorrow, I shall hand him a draft of a constitution. Shall I be successful? Do I want to be successful? The future is black."

There was a second interview on the following day. "Liberty is not exactly what he is after," Benjamin realized. But there was a third interview, and a fourth, and on the 19th he recorded that "many of my constitutional ideas have been adopted." On the 22nd he attended his first meeting as a member of the new Council of State. "If they don't monkey with the constitution, all will be well, but . . . " was the entry in the diary.

"There has been a great victory, so they say," noted the new Councilor of State on June 18. "If that's true, it isn't the whole of the story. If the news is false, then things are worse than anyone could believe."

Forty-eight hours later Benjamin was reading his novel *Adolphe* out loud to Queen Hortense of Holland. "The lack of news about the victory is beginning to be disturbing," he set down in his notebook. "There was, so it seems, a complete collapse on the 18th. May God's will be done."

On the 21st he met with the Emperor in the gardens of the Elysée Palace, and found that he was digesting Waterloo with the utmost calm. "He'll abdicate tomorrow, I imagine," Benjamin concluded.

This might have been the end of Benjamin's political career, but it was not. He wrote a memorable apology for his conduct, and succeeded in convincing Louis XVIII that he had made an honest mistake. "I almost convinced myself," Benjamin is said to have told a friend. His life was sufficiently complicated without the resentment of a king. He had fallen frantically in love with Juliette Récamier, and his relations with Germaine were strained as they had not been since Charlotte's attempted suicide.

As early as the fall of 1814 he had written his cousin Rosalie of the new tension between him and his great friend. "Falling out of love," he reported, "is a little like losing a slice of one's income. A man who would be well off with a thousand shillings a year, if only he had been born a peasant, thinks he is ruined when he is down to ten thousand. In the same way, people who have been very much in love are likely to take a real dislike to each other instead of getting on as everyone else does. Moreover, I have something to complain of, for I no sooner have a chat with a woman in Paris than Madame de Staël starts the rumor that I'm having a new love affair—which is ridiculous for a man of my age, and most embarrassing for a man in my position."

Such was the situation before Germaine made her

plans for the marriage of Albertine to the Duc de Broglie. "He was and is a peer of France," Albertine's mother reminded Thomas Jefferson. "He's the grandson of the marshal, and moreover he is a friend of Lafayette, which says all that needs to be said from the political standpoint. Our family," she concluded, "is like a tiny island of the mind, in which Franklin, Washington, and Jefferson have the same standing they have at home."

The island was undeniably troubled by the passion of Benjamin for Juliette. "Madame de Staël," he concluded, "is a serpent whose vanity is becoming atrocious. The truth is, she hates me, and I feel the same way about her. I must save my income from the claws of that harpy." It was apparent that a real issue was about to be joined; if Albertine were to marry her duke, a dowry was necessary.*

"You know very well what people will say about you," Germaine wrote from Coppet in the spring of 1815. "I am ready," she announced, "to forgive everything except your cold heart. . . . You promised, when my daughter got married, to give me back 40,000 of the 80,000 francs I lent you."

The strain was almost too much for Germaine when seven weeks went by without receiving a draft for the amount. "I don't know how to reply to your last letter," she admitted on the 15th of May. "It's beyond anything I thought possible from a human being. The laws of this country will defend my rights; I shall see my lawyers. But even if I should lose my case, I shall have the bitter pleasure of collecting the documents which won't fail to create the deepest sympathy for a person who was so unfortunate as to have been associated with you for fifteen years. You have the cheek to abuse the gener-

---

* If Benjamin had been malicious he could have reminded Germaine that she had sworn that Albertine must make a "mariage d'inclination."

osity I showed for you in the days when I was in love with you."

She was, she informed her old friend, well aware of the quality of his investments. "I know your portfolio as well as my own. . . . You are richer than I am at the present moment, you have no one to take care of, and you have no obligations of any kind. . . . I am not asking you to do me a favor. You owe me 80,000 francs. Pay half of what you owe me, and let me alone. . . . My advice for you would be for you to be lucky in everything you set out to do from now on, for you would not know how to behave if things went badly."

Five days later she was even angrier. "You are," she wrote, "threatening me with *my letters.* This latest idea of yours is really unworthy of you. Threatening a woman—instead of paying the money you owe her—by releasing letters that could compromise her and her family, that is the one thing that Monsieur de Sade did not think of."

Early in June she returned to the attack. "You have been telling me that for six thousand years now women have been complaining about men who did not love them. But for six thousand years now men have been in love with money, and for the last two months I would say that you have not been exactly indifferent on this point.

"Your relentless hatred has devastated the innermost recesses of my soul. I had begun to think of the old days, but then you had to tell my daughter and me that you had never loved any woman longer than three months, a wretched thing even for a roué to say, and which you might have spared poor innocent Albertine. You, who go around buying up houses, paying for them at the gambling tables, you might have made a small sacrifice for the daughter of the woman who once

210

gave you 80,000 francs, and would give them to you again if she had them."

This was a monologue that eventually came to an end. Reassured by the news that Louis XVIII was willing to repay the loan which Necker made the treasury of France, Germaine abandoned the battle with Benjamin and turned her thoughts to the details of Albertine's wedding. "You have been out of your mind and you have been very cruel," she wrote her old friend. "But after all you have an intellect, and you have a way of saying things like no one else. . . . You can always count on my daughter and me. We shall never be all that we should like to be to you, we can only be what you allowed us to be—merely your friends, and you may one day realize what a priceless thing our friendship is."

On the 15th of February, 1816, Albertine and her duke contracted a civil marriage at Leghorn. Five days later at the Casa Roncioni at Pisa they joined hands, blessed by both a Roman Catholic priest and a Calvinist pastor. Benjamin was present at neither ceremony, but when September came he found he could not forget a certain anniversary. "Twenty-two years ago at this very hour," he put down in his diary, "I saw Madame de Staël for the first time. If I had been wise, I should never have contracted that attachment. If I had been wiser, I should never have severed the connection."

With Benjamin beyond her immediate reach, Germaine took a strong interest in the summer of 1816 in the career of Lord Byron. She did her best to bring about a reconciliation between Byron and his wife, and at times she came close to terrifying the poet. "Poor de Staël!" Byron told Lady Blessington. "She came down upon me like an avalanche, whenever I told her any of my amiable truths, sweeping everything before her with that eloquence that always overwhelmed, but never convinced."

But Byron was entertained. He used to say that "Madame de Staël was certainly the cleverest, though not the most agreeable woman he had ever known . . . there was an obscurity that left the impression that she did not perfectly understand what she endeavored to render intelligible, to others. She *thought* like a man, but alas! she *felt* like a woman."

Germaine may have been "frightful as a precipice," as Byron described her to a Swiss girl, but he greatly enjoyed teasing her at Coppet. He made plain that in his opinion *Delphine* and *Corinne* were "very dangerous productions to be put into the hands of young women." In fact, the virtuous characters in the latter novel were "dull, commonplace, and tedious," and what was this but "a most insidious blow aimed at virtue, and calculated to throw it into the shade."

"She was," Byron reported, "so excited and impatient to attempt a refutation that it was only by my volubility that I could keep her silent. She interrupted me every moment by gesticulating, exclaiming *Quelle idée! Mon Dieu! Ecoutez donc! Vous m'impatientez!* . . . I was ready to laugh outright at the idea that I, who was at that period considered the most *mauvais sujet* of the day, should give Madame de Staël a lecture on morals, and I knew that this added to her rage." But Byron, for all his impertinence, was a relief from callers who took Germaine too seriously. There were earnest souls who spoke of three powers in Europe: Russia, England, and Madame de Staël.

Respected she was, but she was never respectful. Back in Paris at the beginning of 1817, she was her vehement self until one February evening, at a ball at the house of Louis XVIII's minister the Duc Decazes, she fainted on the staircase. She was brought home, paralyzed. Her greatest comfort in the days to come was Rocca, who never left her bedside. She was, she murmured, afraid of falling asleep and of never seeing Rocca again, and would take a nap only if he promised to wake her up at the end of five or ten minutes.

Yet there were visitors whom she prized, and no one more than Chateaubriand. "One morning I went to see her in the rue Royale," he recalled in his memoirs. "The blinds were pulled two thirds of the way down. The bed, set against the wall in the back of the room, left only space to turn around on the left. The curtains were drawn back, forming two columns at the head of the bed. There was Madame de Staël propped up by pillows. I drew near, and once I was accustomed to the darkness, I made out the ailing woman. Her cheeks were flushed with fever. Her eyes met mine in the dusk, and she said: *Good morning, my dear Francis. I am suffering, but that can't prevent me from being as fond of you as ever.* She held out her hand. I took it and kissed it. When I looked up, I perceived something white and peaked on the other side of her. It was Monsieur Rocca, whose face was wan, whose cheeks were hollow, whose eyes were strained, and whose complexion was ravaged. There was no doubt he was a dying man. I had never seen him before; I was never to see him again. He did not say a word, but he bowed to me as he passed by. His footsteps were inaudible; he was as fleeting as a shadow. For a second he stopped at the door to take his leave. The two ghosts sent a shiver down my spine as I watched them stare at each other in silence. He could stand up straight but he was deathly pale. Her cheeks were so brilliant that my heart failed me."

This, apparently, was the last time that Germaine looked on Chateaubriand. But she thought of him constantly in these days. She scribbled a message to him in the last letter she wrote, and she summed up for him her conception of herself. "I have," she told him, "always been the same, no matter what happened. I have loved God, my father, and liberty."

In her generosity she made a point, despite doctor's orders, of receiving a gentleman whom she had never seen before. This was George Ticknor from Boston, the young Dartmouth graduate who was about to lay the foundations of the department of romance languages at Harvard. Ticknor was in deadly earnest, but his ambition was pleasing to Germaine. He had read *De l'Allemagne*, and could not rest until he had crossed the Rhine and mastered the language. The Germans, he confided to a friend, "are a people who, in forty years, have created to themselves a literature such as no other nation ever created in two centuries; and they are a people who, at this moment, have more mental activity than any other existing." It was no wonder he considered his trip to Europe "a sacrifice of enjoyment to improvement."

Ticknor admitted that August Wilhelm von Schlegel "talked to me about his Sanscrit a little more than I cared to have him, but that is the privilege of age." He was not so pleased with August Wilhelm's brother Friedrich. "Never," he wrote, "was I more disappointed in the external appearance of any man in my life; for, instead of finding one grown spare and dry with deep and wearisome study, I found before me a short, thick little gentleman with the ruddy, vulgar health of a full-fed father of the church."

Ticknor was happier in the presence of Goethe, still happier in the presence of Germaine. "She was," Ticknor testified, "in bed, pale, feeble, and evidently depressed in spirits; and the mere stretching out of her hand to me, or rather, making a slight movement, as if she had desired to do it, cost an effort that was painful to witness.

"Observing," Ticknor went on, "with that intuition for which she has always been famous, the effect her situation produced on me, she said: *Il ne faut pas me juger de ce que vous voyez ici. Ce n'est pas moi, ce n'est que l'ombre de ce que j'étais il y a quatre mois— et une ombre qui peut-être disparaîtra bientôt.* I told her that Monsieur Portal and her other physicians did not think so. *Oui,* said she, while her eye kindled in the consciousness that she was about to say one of those brilliant things with which she had so often electrified a drawing-room, *oui, je sais, mais ils y mettent toujours tant de vanité d'auteur que je ne m'y fie pas du tout. Je ne me relèverai jamais de cette maladie.*

"She saw at this moment that the Duchesse de Broglie had entered the apartment and was so much affected by the last remark, that she had gone to the window to hide her feelings. She therefore began to talk about America. . . . *Vous êtes l'avant-garde du genre humain, vous êtes l'avenir du monde.* . . . There came a light tinge of feeling into her face, which spoke plainly enough of the pride of genius. As I feared to weary her with conversation, I asked her daughter if I should not go; but she said she was glad to see her mother interested, and wished rather that I should stay. I remained therefore half an hour longer, until dinner was announced, during which we talked chiefly of the prospects of Europe, of which she despairs. "When I rose to go, she gave me her hand, and said, under the impression I was soon going to America: *Vous serez bientôt chez vous—et moi j'y vais aussi.* I pretended not to understand her, and told her I was sure I should see her in Switzerland, much better. She looked on her daughter, while her eyes filled with tears, and said in English, *God grant me that favor,* and I left her."

Germaine was not deceived. At 51 she was near the end, so near that the Duc de Broglie had her removed to a house in the rue Neuve-des-Mathurins, where there was a garden into which she was trundled every afternoon in a wheel chair. There were, of course, moments of hope. She once turned to the Duc d'Orléans, who had come to call, and hinted she might spend the next winter in Naples.

On the night of July 13 Germaine found it impossible to sleep, and she asked Miss Randall, who had come to stay with her, for a dose of opium. The dose was refused, then finally given. "Now, won't you go to sleep?" asked Miss Randall. "I'll sleep as soundly as any old peasant woman," was the answer.

At five o'clock in the morning of July 14, 1817, Miss Randall woke up and went to feel Germaine's hands. They were like ice. The Duc de Broglie was summoned; he understood. He notified Schlegel and Rocca and he went at once in search of Benjamin Constant, who was, said the Duke, "deeply moved."

This was a generous remark of the Duke. He suspected that Constant was a deist—or no better than an atheist—and he was appalled by the indiscretions made public in *Adolphe*. He had, the Duke admitted in his memoirs, no use for novels, and *Adolphe* was a particularly reprehensible specimen. He had once listened to Constant read the work out loud, and had been embarrassed, first by the tears of the audience when he came to the end, and then by the hysterical laughter in which the author joined.

But the Duke understood that it was his duty to put up with Benjamin. He invited him to the funeral chapel in Paris, and the two sat down side by side to watch over the body. Later on, after the services in Geneva, Benjamin and his wife rode in the front of the carriage that brought the coffin to the mausoleum at Coppet. And when the coffin was set down next to the bodies of her father and mother, Benjamin followed Auguste de Staël into the crypt for the last glance.

The mausoleum was then sealed, never to be re-opened.

When the will was read, there were no real surprises, although Germaine did choose to reveal that she had been secretly married to Rocca. "I have," she declared in the document, "only one piece of advice to give my children, and that is to keep constantly in mind the moral standards of my father, and to try to imitate him at all times, each in his own way according to his own abilities. I have never known anyone in this world who could be compared to my father, and with every day of my life my respect for him and my love for him have become more and more a part of my character." *

"Take her all in all," Benjamin Constant reflected, "you'll never see the like of her again." Albert Gallatin, the American minister at the court of Louis XVIII, was inclined to agree. He had had many letters from Germaine on the subject of her American investments, and he could comprehend an aspect of her character that might have escaped her lover. "Her mind," Gallatin informed Thomas Jefferson, "improved with the years without any diminution of her fine and brilliant genius. She was a power by herself and had more influence on public opinion and even on the acts of government than any other person not in the ministry. I may add that she was one of your sincere admirers."

Although Marcel Proust compared Coppet to a church become a national monument, but a church in which Mass is still said, the final tribute to Germaine was composed by Chateaubriand, who made his way to

---

* Necker could have had no reason to complain of the descendants of Victor and Albertine de Broglie. The line has been distinguished. Their grandson Maurice Duc de Broglie was one of the outstanding nuclear physicists of the twentieth century. His brother Louis Victor de Broglie won the Nobel prize for physics in 1929.

Coppet in 1832 in the company of Juliette Récamier.

Coppet was closed on the day that Chateaubriand and Madame Récamier arrived, but the two of them gained admittance and wandered through the empty apartments. When Juliette went into what had once been her own bedroom, memories crowded upon her: she half expected to find Germaine at the piano in the drawing-room.

They went into the park, where Juliette walked up and down the paths she had followed so many times with her great friend. Then she went alone to look upon the mausoleum, concealed a few steps away in a thicket.

"I sat down on a bench to wait for her," Chateaubriand remembered. "I turned my back on France; I had my eyes fixed on Lake Geneva. There were thick clouds on the horizon behind the dark line of the peaks of the Jura. . . . On the other side of the lake I could make out Lord Byron's house, whose roof was lit up by the setting sun. Rousseau was no longer with us to admire this sight; Voltaire, too, was gone, whose eyes had never rested on such things. It was then that I thought of the great dead on our side of the lake come to pay their respects to Madame de Staël: they seemed to be searching for their peer in the other world, so that they might rise to heaven with her and keep her company in the night.

"At that moment Madame Récamier, pale and weeping, came out of the funereal grove, looking very like a visitor from beyond. If I ever understood the vanity of glory and the the truth of life, it was when I gazed at that dark and silent wood where she sleeps who was so brilliant and so famous, for it was then that I comprehended what it meant to be truly loved."

ACKNOWLEDGMENTS

BIBLIOGRAPHY

INDEX

ACKNOWLEDGMENTS

No author of a book about Madame de Staël could possibly overlook the devotion and generosity of her descendants, who have not only immeasurably enriched the literature on the subject, but also have gone to no end of trouble to be helpful to scholars from all parts of the world who have attempted to survey her career. I can never forget the great kindness of the Comtesse Jean de Pange, who on the very eve of her husband's death consented to receive my wife and me. Nor can I forget the welcome of the Comtesse d'Andlau, who made possible our visit to Coppet and to Chateaubriand's birthplace at Combourg.

I should also be most ungrateful if I failed to mention the late J. Lestrohan, the great teacher who many years ago introduced me to the riches of the French language. In more recent times Dr. Joseph P. Bauke of Columbia University has been a perfect guide in my exploration of German. I am indebted to him for his careful reading of this book and for countless pertinent suggestions.

I should also like to thank A. K. Placzek of Avery Library for his reading of the Weimar chapter, and Johannes Urzidil for his thoughtfulness in tracing a Goethe quotation incorrectly cited by Thomas Mann. Much of the research for this book was made easier by the resources of the New York Society Library, which made available to me the standard edition of Madame de Staël's works, published in Paris in seventeen volumes, 1820 and 1821.

Andlau, B. d'. *Madame de Staël*. Geneva, 1960.

Argenson, Marquis d'. "Une Amie de Madame de Staël," *Revue de France* (June 1, 1927).

Baille, Charles. "Notes sur le Baron et la Baronne de Staël," *Revue de Paris* (April, 1902).

Balayé, Simone (ed.). Madame de Staël: *Lettres à Ribbing*. Paris, 1960.

Baldensperger, F. (ed.). "Lettres inédites de Zacharias Werner à Madame de Staël," *Revue de Littérature Comparée* (January-March, 1923).

Barante, C. de (ed.). *Souvenirs du Baron de Barante*. 5 vols. Paris, 1890-95.

Barras, Paul-François, Vicomte de. *Mémoires*. Paris, 1906.

Barrett, Charlotte Frances (ed.). *The Diary and Letters of Madame D'Arblay*, 7 vols. London, 1842-46.

Bastian, Maurice. *Madame de Staël et l'Allemagne*. Geneva, 1939.

Beauverd, Pierre. *Coppet*. Neuchâtel, 1949.

Berthoud, Dorette. *Constance et grandeur de Benjamin Constant*. Lausanne, 1944.

————. *La Seconde Madame Benjamin Constant*. Paris, 1943.

Beutler, Ernst (ed.). Goethe: *Gedenkausgabe*. 24 vols. Zurich, 1948-54.

Bezard, Yvonne. *Madame de Staël d'après ses portraits*. Paris, 1938.

Blennerhassett, Charlotte Julia von Leyden, Lady. *Madame de Staël*. 3 vols. London, 1889.

Blöcking, E. (ed.). A. W. von Schlegel: *Gesammelte Werke*. 12 vols. Leipzig, 1846-47.

Boigne, Charlotte-Louise-Eléonore, Comtesse de. *Mémoires*. 2 vols. Paris, 1907.

Bonald, Louis-Gabriel-Ambroise, Vicomte de. *Observations sur l'ouvrage de Madame de Staël ayant pour titre: Considérations sur les principaux évènements de la révolution française*. Paris, 1818.

Bonstetten, Karl Viktor von. *Briefe an Friederike Brun.* 2 vols. Frankfurt am Main, 1829.

Broglie, Achille-Charles-Léonce-Victor, Duc de. *Souvenirs du feu Duc de Broglie.* 4 vols. Paris, 1886.

Broglie, Jacques, Prince de. *Madame de Staël et sa cour au château de Chaumont.* Paris, 1936.

Buchwald, Reinhard (ed.). *Friedrich Schillers Briefe.* Leipzig, n. d.

————. *Schiller: Leben und Werk.* Wiesbaden, 1959.

Chinard, Gilbert (ed.). "La Correspondance de Madame de Staël avec Jefferson," *Revue de Littérature Comparée* (October-December, 1922).

Croce, Benedetto. *Uomini e cose della vecchia Italia.* Bari, 1927.

Dard, Emile. *Un Confident de l'Empereur: Le Comte de Narbonne.* Paris, 1943.

Davenport, Beatrice Cary (ed.). Gouverneur Morris: *A Diary of the French Revolution.* 2 vols. Boston, 1939.

Dax d'Axat, Marquis de. "Souvenirs sur Madame de Staël," *Revue de Paris* (July 1, 1933).

Dejob, Charles. *Madame de Staël et l'Italie.* Paris, 1890.

Du Bos, Charles. *Grandeur et misère de Benjamin Constant.* Paris, 1946.

Faure, H. "Madame de Staël et le Duc de Palmella," *La Revue* (August 15, 1903).

Gautier, Paul (ed.). "Lettres de Madame de Staël au Roi Joseph," *Revue des Deux Mondes* (December 15, 1936 and January 15, 1937).

————. *Mathieu de Montmorency et Madame de Staël.* Paris, 1908.

————. *Madame de Staël et Napoléon.* Paris, 1903.

————. "Madame de Staël et la république en 1798," *Revue des Deux Mondes* (November 15, 1921).

————. "Le Premier Exil de Madame de Staël," *Revue des Deux Mondes* (December, 1906).

Geffroy, A. *Gustave III et la Cour de France.* 2 vols. Paris, 1867.

Genlis, Stéphane-Félicité du Crest de Saint-Aubin, Marquise de. *De l'Influence des femmes sur la littérature française.* Paris, 1811.

————. *Mémoires.* Paris, 1885.

Gérando, Gustave, Baron de (ed.). *Lettres inédites et souvenirs biographiques de Madame Récamier et de Madame de Staël.* Paris, 1868.

Gibbon, Edward. *Autobiographies.* London, 1896.

Goetze, Alfred. *Ein Fremder Gast: Frau von Staël in Deutschland 1803-04.* Jena, 1928.

Grimm, Hermann. *Das Leben Goethes.* Stuttgart, 1960.

Guillemin, Henri. *Madame de Staël, Benjamin Constant et Napoléon.* Paris, 1959.

Gunnell, Doris. "Madame de Staël en Angleterre," *Revue d'Histoire Littéraire de la France* (December, 1913).

Haussonville, Gabriel-Paul-Othenin de Cléon, Comte d'. *Madame de Staël et l'Allemagne.* Paris, 1928.

————. *Madame de Staël et Monsieur Necker d'après leur correspondance inédite.* Paris, 1925.

————. *Le Salon de Madame Necker.* 2 vols. Paris, 1882.

Hawkins, Richmond L. *Madame de Staël and the United States.* Cambridge, 1930.

Hemlow, Joyce. *The History of Fanny Burney.* New York, 1958.

Henning, Ian Allen. *L'Allemagne de Madame de Staël et la polémique romantique.* Paris, 1929.

Herold, J. Christopher. *Mistress to an Age: A Life of Madame de Staël.* New York, 1958.

Herriot, Edouard. *Madame Récamier et ses amis.* Paris, 1934.

Hill, Constance. *Juniper Hall.* London, 1904.

Hillard, G. S. (ed.). George Ticknor, Jr.: *Life, Letters and Journal.* 2 vols. Boston, 1876.

Hitzig, J. E. (ed.). A. von Chamisso: *Gesammelte Werke.* 6 vols. Berlin, 1864.

Jaeck, Emma Gertrude. *Madame de Staël and the Spread of German Literature.* New York, 1915.

Jasinski, Béatrice W. (ed.). *Madame de Staël: Lettres inédites à Louis de Narbonne.* Paris, 1960.

Kluth, O. "Madame de Staël et le Baron Voght," *Occident et Cahiers Staëliens* (October, 1939).

Knapton, Ernest John. *The Lady of the Holy Alliance: The Life of Julie de Krüdener.* New York, 1939.

Kohler, Pierre. *Madame de Staël au château de Coppet.* Lausanne, 1928.

————. *Madame de Staël et la Suisse.* Lausanne, 1916.

Köster, Albert (ed.). *Briefe der Frau Rat Goethe.* Wiesbaden, 1956.

Küster, Heinrich. *Die Politische Rolle der Frau von Staël in der Französichen Revolution.* Greifswald, 1931.

Lacour-Gayet, G. *Talleyrand.* 4 vols. Paris, 1930-34.

Lacretelle, Pierre de. *Madame de Staël et les hommes.* Paris, 1939.

Lanfredini, Dina. "Madame de Staël e i suoi amici italiani," *Rivista di Letteratura Moderne* (June and December, 1946; September and December, 1947).

————. "Le Secret de Corinne: Oswald et Prosper de Barante," *Occident et Cahiers Staëliens* (February 15, 1935).

Lang, André. *Une Vie d'orages: Germaine de Staël.* Paris, 1958.

Larg, David Glass. *Madame de Staël: La Seconde Vie (1800-07).* Paris, 1928.

————. *Madame de Staël: La Vie dans l'oeuvre (1766-1800).* Paris, 1924.

Lavaquerry, E. *Necker: Fourrier de la révolution.* Paris, 1933.

Le Marois, Comtesse (ed.). "Lettres à Monsieur de Staël," *Revue des Deux Mondes* (June 15 and July 1, 1932; March 1, March 15, and April 1, 1939).

Levaillant, Maurice. *Une Amitié amoureuse: Madame de Staël et Madame Récamier.* Paris, 1956.

————. *Les Amours de Benjamin Constant.* Paris, 1958.

————, and Moulinier, Georges (eds.). Chateaubriand: *Mémoires d'outre-tombe.* 2 vols. Paris, 1946.

Loménie, Emmanuel Beau de (ed.). *Lettres de Madame de Staël à Madame Récamier.* Paris, 1952.

Loménie, Louis-Léonard de (ed.). Benjamin Constant: *Lettres à Madame Récamier.* Paris, 1882.

Marchant, Leslie A. *Byron: A Biography.* 3 vols. New York, 1957.

Menos, Jean-H. (ed.). *Lettres de Benjamin Constant à sa famille.* Paris, 1931.

Michelet, Jules. *Les Femmes de la révolution.* Paris, 1854.

Mistler, Jean (ed.). *Lettres à un ami par Benjamin Con-*

stant et *Madame de Staël: Cent Onze Lettres inédites à Claude Hochet*. Neuchâtel, 1949.

Mistler, Jean. *Madame de Staël et Maurice O'Donnell*. Paris, 1926.

Mistral d'Auriol, Jean. "Madame de Staël et la Police Autrichienne en 1812," *La Vie des Peuples* (July, 1924).

Monti, Giovanni and Achille (eds.). *Lettere Inédite del Foscolo, del Giordani et della Signora di Staël a Vincenzo Monti*. Leghorn, 1876.

Necker, Albertine-Adrienne de Saussure. *Notice sur le caractère et les écrits de Madame de Staël*. Paris, 1820.

Nicolson, Harold. *Benjamin Constant*. London, 1949.

Nolde, Baronne de (ed.). *Lettres de Madame de Staël à Benjamin Constant*. Paris, 1928.

Norton, J. E. (ed.). *The Letters of Edward Gibbon*. 3 vols. New York, 1956.

Norvins, J. de. *Mémorial*. 2 vols. Paris, 1896.

Oehlenschläger, Adam. *Meine Lebenserinnerungen*. 2 vols. Leipzig, 1850.

Oliver, J. W. *The Life of William Beckford*. New York, 1932.

Pange, Pauline-Laure-Marie de Broglie, Comtesse Jean de. *Auguste-Guillaume Schlegel et Madame de Staël*. Paris, 1938.

————. *Le Dernier Amour de Madame de Staël*. Geneva, 1944.

———— (ed.). Madame de Staël: *De l'Allemagne*. 5 vols. Paris, 1958-60.

————. *Madame de Staël et la découverte de l'Allemagne*. Paris, 1929.

————. "Madame de Staël et les Etats-Unis," *Revue de Paris* (September 1, 1933).

————. *Madame de Staël et François de Pange*. Paris, 1925.

————. "Madame de Staël et le Prince de Ligne," *Annales Prince de Ligne*, Vol. XVI (1935).

————. *Monsieur de Staël*. Paris, 1931.

————. "Un Voyage de Madame de Staël en Europe Centrale," *Nouvelle Revue de Hongrie* (April, 1941).

Pange, Victor de (ed.). *Madame de Staël et le Duc de Wellington: Correspondence inédite 1815-17.* Paris, 1962.

Pellegrini, Carlo. *Madame de Staël—Il Gruppo Cosmopolito di Coppet—L'Influenza delle sue idee critiche.* Florence, 1938.

Porta, Maria Teresa. *Madame de Staël e l'Italia.* Florence, 1910.

Proust, Marcel. *Chroniques.* Paris, 1927.

Reichardt, Johann Friedrich. *Vertraute Briefe aus Paris geschrieben in den Jahren 1802 und 1803.* 2 vols. Hamburg, 1805.

Reval, Gabrielle. "Le Secret de Corinne: Oswald et le Duc de Palmella," *Occident et Cahiers Staëliens* (February 15, 1935).

Rodocanchi, E. "Madame Récamier et Madame de Staël," *Revue Politique et Littéraire* (September 15, 1928).

Roulin, Alfred and Suzanne (eds.). Benjamin et Rosalie de Constant: *Correspondence.* Paris, 1953.

Roulin, Alfred (ed.). *Oeuvres de Benjamin Constant.* Paris, 1957.

Rudler, Gustave. *La Jeunesse de Benjamin Constant.* Paris, 1908.

———— (ed.). Madame de Staël: *Lettres inédites à Juste Constant de Rebeque.* Paris, 1937.

Russell, Lord John (ed.). Thomas Moore: *Memoirs, Journal and Correspondence.* 8 vols. London, 1853.

Sadler, Thomas (ed.). Henry Crabb Robinson: *Diary, Reminiscences and Correspondence.* 2 vols. Boston, 1869.

Sainte-Beuve, Charles-Augustin. *Causeries du Lundi.* 16 vols. Paris, n. d.

————. *Portraits de Femmes.* Paris, n. d.

————. *Portraits littéraires.* 3 vols. Paris, n. d.

Schermerhorn, Elizabeth. *Benjamin Constant.* Boston, 1929.

Schlegel, August Wilhelm von. *Essais littéraires et historiques.* Bonn, 1842.

Scott, Geoffrey. *The Portrait of Zélide.* With an introduction by George Dangerfield. New York, 1959.

Solovieff, Georges (ed.). Madame de Staël: *Lettres à Narbonne*. Paris, 1960.

Sorel, Albert. *Madame de Staël*. Paris, 1890.

Sparks, Jared. *The Life of Gouverneur Morris*. 3 vols. Boston, 1832.

Staël, Auguste de (ed.). *Oeuvres complètes de Monsieur Necker*. 15 vols. Paris, 1820.

Staël-Holstein, Anne-Louise-Germaine Necker, Baronne de (ed.). *Manuscrits de Monsieur Necker*. Paris, 1804.

Taillandier, Saint-René (ed.). *Lettres inédites de J.-C.-L. de Sismondi, de Monsieur Bonstetten, de Madame de Staël et de Madame de Souza à Madame la Comtesse d'Albany*. Paris, 1863.

Talleyrand-Périgord, Charles-Maurice de. *Mémoires*. 7 vols. Paris, 1906.

Ustéri, Paul, and Rittger, Eugène (eds.). *Lettres inédites de Madame de Staël à Henri Meister*. Paris, 1903.

Viatte, Auguste. *Les Sources occultes du romantisme*. 2 vols. Paris, 1928.

Villemaret, M. de (ed.). Bourrienne: *Mémoires*. 10 vols. Paris, 1831.

Whitford, Robert C. *Madame de Staël's Literary Reputation in England*. Urbana, 1918.

Wittmer, Louis. *Charles de Villers*. Paris, 1908.

INDEX